Contents

Why you should read this book   v
Who is this book for?   v
What will I need?   vi
Features of the book   vi
ECDL   viii
What you should know   ix

Part One: Using PowerPoint   1

1   **My first PowerPoint presentation**   3
In the beginning   3
Getting on with it   9
What you should know   19

2   **Making it more interesting**   21
Beyond printed OHPs   21
Making it look prettier   22
Formatting for the whole presentation   29
Animation effects   39
What you should know   51

3   **Adding graphics, tables, charts, audio and video**   53
A new scenario   53
Organisational charts   66
Inserting a table   71
Introducing graphs   80
Adding photos to your presentation   86
Adding lines, boxes and text boxes to your presentation   90
Sound and video   96

Finishing touches 99
What you should know 99

4 Setting up a house style 101
What is a house style? 101
How to set up a house style 101
NHS house styles 105
What you should know 107

5 PowerPoint and the World Wide Web 109
Using the World Wide Web as a source of material 109
Using the World Wide Web as a publishing medium 122
What you should know 129

Part Two: Talking and using PowerPoint 131

6 How not to ruin a presentation with PowerPoint 133
Introduction 133
Avoiding mistakes: follow the information highway code 133
Some good things to do 140
What you should know 144

7 Talking with PowerPoint 145
Why use PowerPoint at all? 145
Why I think many talks with PowerPoint are so boring 145
Planning a presentation with PowerPoint 147
Giving a presentation with PowerPoint 151
PowerPoint checklist 152
What you should know 154

8 The PowerPoint gallery: examples of presentations 155
Sample presentation 1 155
Sample presentation 2 158
What you should know 169

9 Party time! 171
The use of party tricks 171
The black screen 171
The curtain call 173
A more sophisticated list 183

10 What's on the CD 187

Index 189

Powerpoint® is a registered trademark of the Microsoft Corporation.

Why you should read this book

Who is this book for?

This book is for healthcare workers who really don't fancy all this technology. It is not for absolute beginners. For that, try *Excel for Clinical Governance* (another of my books, and currently my best seller). It assumes that you can use Windows, a mouse and know what a menu is (a collection of delicious food? Wrong answer – go to *Excel for Clinical Governance*, do not pass GO, do not collect £200).

However, it is intended to be readable, approachable and not to assume prior knowledge of PowerPoint. A typical reader might be one of the following.

- You have to give presentations to colleagues and feel left out when you're still using hand-drawn overheads.
- You have completed early modules of the ECDL and are now looking at the presentation module and want a bit of help.
- You have completed all the ECDL and want to see how to apply it in a clinical context.
- You think that ECDL stands for Every Computer Deserves Lashing (actually it's the European Computer Driving Licence and the NHS is adopting it as a base IT qualification (-ish!)) but want to use PowerPoint to help you with a presentation. You should ignore the 'ECDL' section of this preface!
- You're a clinician and you're fed up with not understanding a word that your daughters/IT people tell you.
- You're a student of ours and need help with the practical work on the technology module.

Whoever you are, if you've got this far, welcome and please read on . . .

What will I need?

You will need access to a PC, with Microsoft Office XP or PowerPoint XP or later. I have used PowerPoint XP as, thanks to a recent deal by Microsoft with the NHS, many of you will have this version by the time you read this. If you have an earlier version, then either upgrade or enjoy the majority of the book where the version makes little difference.

This book comes with a CD which will also take you out into the wonderful world of the World Wide Web. Therefore it is certainly advantageous to have a CD-ROM drive and Internet access.

CD link
From the CD accompanying this book you can download a range of useful but not quite essential items. It will at times also link through to the World Wide Web.

Features of the book

One of the main distinctive features of the book is **Smart Alec**:

Smart Alec says
'Let me introduce myself. My name is Smart Alec and I am his (the author's) *alter ego*. I pop up throughout the text and throw in the asides that he would if he was teaching. Sometimes I just heckle him to keep up the interest level. It is alleged that some of you may find my presence irritating at times; if so, just ignore me, and I'll return the compliment. And despite rumours to the contrary I do not wear an anorak.'

Alec's bits are designed to help, but they are not essential: if you don't find them helpful then ignore them.

Smart Alec says
'Thanks very much.'

See what I mean?

Another key feature is the 'Over to you' section.

Over to you
These sections cover practical activities for you to do.

They are tasks to undertake when you have already worked through a very similar task in the main text. They serve to reinforce and to build up confidence.

Finally, as you work through the text you will build up a presentation. This is meant to help you understand what on earth is going on!

As you gain more confidence, the explanations do become a little sparser. If you find yourself getting a little lost, try slowing down a bit. Similarly, if you find the explanations becoming wearisome, then go and talk to my *alter ego*!

ECDL

In the table below, I have shown how the learning outcomes of ECDL are covered within this book.

ECDL knowledge area	Sub-section	Covered in Chapter
6.1 Getting started	6.1.1 First Steps with Presentation Tools	Assumed knowledge. Covered in *Excel for Clinical Governance*, which also covers spreadsheets in greater detail than ECDL requires for module 4
	6.1.2 Adjust Basic Settings	Assumed knowledge. Covered in *Excel for Clinical Governance*
	6.1.3 Document Exchange	Assumed knowledge. Covered in *Excel for Clinical Governance*, except for web operations covered in Chapter 5
6.2 Basic operations	6.2.1 Create a Presentation	Chapter 1
	6.2.2 Copy, Move, Delete – Text	Chapter 2
	6.2.3 Copy, Move, Delete – Images	Chapter 3
	6.2.4 Copy, Move, Delete – Slides	Chapter 3
6.3 Formatting	6.3.1 Format Text	Chapter 2
	6.3.2 Modify Text Boxes	Chapter 3
6.4 Graphics and charts	6.4.1 Drawn Objects	Chapter 3
	6.4.2 Charts	
	6.4.3 Images & Other Objects	
6.5 Printing and distribution	6.5.1 Slide Setup	Chapter 4
	6.5.2 Prepare for Distribution	Chapter 5
	6.5.3 Printing	Chapter 1
6.6 Slide show effects	6.6.1 Preset Animation	Chapter 2
	6.6.2 Transitions	Chapter 2
6.7 View a slide show	6.7.1 Delivering a Presentation	Chapter 1

However, this book also tries to help you use PowerPoint to make your presentations more effective.

Smart Alec says

'What he really means is that he's fed up of sitting through really boring presentations where people have forgotten to think about what they're saying and simply read out a load of bullet points off a PowerPoint presentation. He'd be really upset if someone did one of those and then said they learned all their PowerPoint skills from this book.'

What you should know

At the end of each chapter, you will find a 'What you should know' section.

And finally, I think PowerPoint can be one of the most enjoyable packages to use, so I hope that at least some of this will be fun!

Alan Gillies
November 2002

powerpoint@alangillies.com

For Anna

Part One:
Using PowerPoint

1

My first PowerPoint presentation

In the beginning

When you first switch on PowerPoint, particularly in its latest incarnation, it can be a bit bewildering. The initial screen should look something like this:

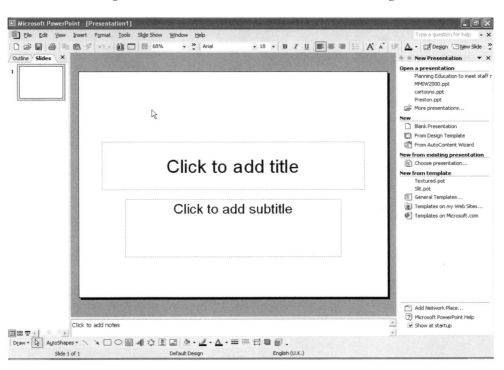

The screen may be thought of as having a number of zones arranged around the main window:

'Zone'	Function
Title bar	The application and file name appear here.
Menu bar	The drop-down menus appear here.
Toolbar	The toolbar provides quick ways of doing things that you use a lot. There's probably one at the bottom as well.
Outline panel	This provides an outline view of the presentation. In the latest version this may be text or graphic.
Shortcut panel	This panel provides more shortcuts to things you want to do and change according to what you're working on.
Main window	This is where the slides themselves appear.
Status bar	The status bar has information on slide number, language, etc.
System taskbar	This isn't part of PowerPoint, but of the Windows operating system itself, and tells you what applications you've got running.

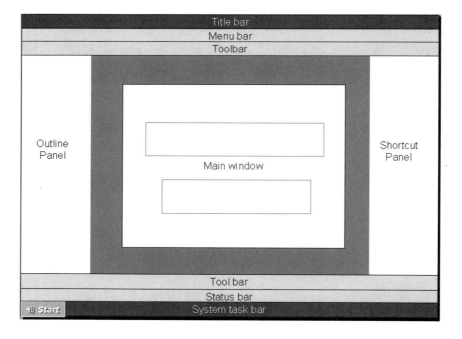

Smart Alec says
'Every time Microsoft brings out a new version, they add more 'usability' features to make it easier to use. Sometimes it just seems to make things more complicated. If you've seen older versions of PowerPoint, you'll know what I mean.

Whilst I'm here, I thought you might like to know that the underlined letters on the menu bar enable you to call up that menu from the keyboard by pressing [ALT] and the letter. Thus . . .

[ALT] and F gets you the File menu. If you then type A, you get the Save as dialog box . . .

Bye for now!'

CD link
The menus and toolbars are nearly uniform across all Office applications, so if you know Word or Excel, you can skip the next bit. If you don't, you'll find the menu layouts reproduced in Acrobat format on the CD. You may like to print them out and keep them handy until you find your way around. Not least because Windows has a habit of hiding things it doesn't think you want. Scary, eh?

If you see the double-headed arrow symbol at the bottom of a menu then it means that there are commands you haven't used for a while. If you wait around long enough, PowerPoint will reveal them.

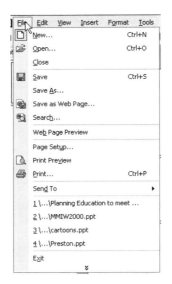

The full menus are shown below.

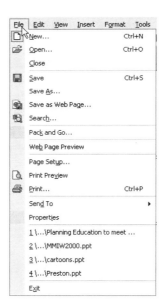

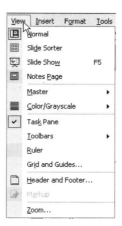

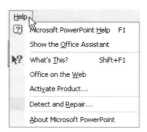

Smart Alec says
'Where there's a toolbar button or a keyboard shortcut, they appear on the menus too. However, what confuses him is that you can't use the keyboard shortcut whilst the menu is open. Still, he's easily confused . . .'

Anyway, better get on with it or Alec will be telling me you're all bored already.

Getting on with it

Throughout the book we're going to use a range of scenarios. The first scenario is that you're a practice manager and you've done an audit on smoking cessation in your practice and you want to present the findings to the partners. You have mapped on paper how you would present it using overheads, and they look like this:

Audit of smoking cessation in line with the CHD NSF

Practice Manager
Haybad Medical Centre
Grimtown

Aim of study

- To investigate the quality of our smoking cessation programme against national standards

Objectives of recording

- The number and proportion of the practice population whose current smoking status is known
- The number and proportion of people recorded as current smokers (i.e. who have smoked a cigarette in the last month)

Objectives of clinic

- The number of smokers newly referred to a smoking cessation clinic in the past year

- The number and proportion of smokers attending a specialist smoking cessation clinic who are not smoking a year after their first attendance at the clinic

Source: CHD NSF (1999)

Results for our practice

- 35% of males with smoking status recorded in last 12 months
- 60% of females with BP recorded in last 3 years
- 45% of males screened are current smokers
- 38% of females screened are current smokers

Results for our practice

- 50 smokers have attended clinic in last 12 months
- Of these, 18 are currently not smoking

Proposed actions

- Implement computerised protocol to check smoking status
- Expand smoking cessation clinic

To start producing this as a PowerPoint presentation,

🖰 Click on the Outline tab

and you can start typing your presentation:

⌨ Type 'Audit of smoking cessation in line with the CHD NSF'
⌨ Press [Tab]
⌨ Type 'Practice Manager', then ↵
⌨ Type 'Haybad Medical Centre' then ↵
⌨ Type 'Grimtown' then ↵

Your first slide is now complete, and the screen should look like this:

To enter the next slide, you need to return to the heading level. To do this:

⌨ Press ⇧ and [Tab] together.

A new slide will appear in the outline:

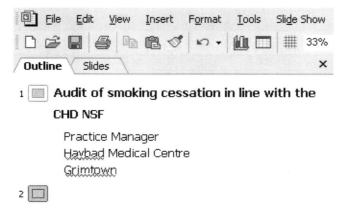

Now complete the presentation in the same way:

- Type 'Aim of study', then ↵
- Press [Tab]
- Type 'To investigate the quality of our smoking cessation programme against national standards', then ↵
- Press ⇧ and [Tab] together.
- Type 'Objectives of recording', then ↵
- Press [Tab]
- Type 'The number and proportion of the practice population whose current smoking status is known', then ↵
- Type 'The number and proportion of people recorded as current smokers (i.e. who have smoked a cigarette in the last month)', then ↵
- Press ⇧ and [Tab] together.
- Type 'Objectives of clinic', then ↵
- Press [Tab]
- Type 'The number of smokers newly referred to a smoking cessation clinic in the past year', then ↵
- Type 'The number and proportion of smokers attending a specialist smoking cessation clinic who are not smoking a year after their first attendance at the clinic', then ↵
- Type 'Source: CHD NSF (1999)', then ↵
- Press ⇧ and [Tab] together.
- Type 'Results for our practice', then ↵
- Press [Tab]
- Type '35% of males with smoking status recorded in last 12 months', then ↵
- Type '60% of females with BP recorded in last 3 years', then ↵
- Type '45% of males screened are current smokers', then ↵
- Type '38% of females screened are current smokers', then ↵
- Press ⇧ and [Tab] together.
- Type 'Results for our practice', then ↵
- Press [Tab]
- Type '50 smokers have attended clinic in last 12 months', then ↵
- Type 'Of these, 18 are currently not smoking', then ↵
- Press ⇧ and [Tab] together.
- Type 'Proposed actions', then ↵
- Press [Tab]
- Type 'Implement computerised protocol to check smoking status', then ↵
- Type 'Expand smoking cessation clinic'.

When you have finished it should look something like this:

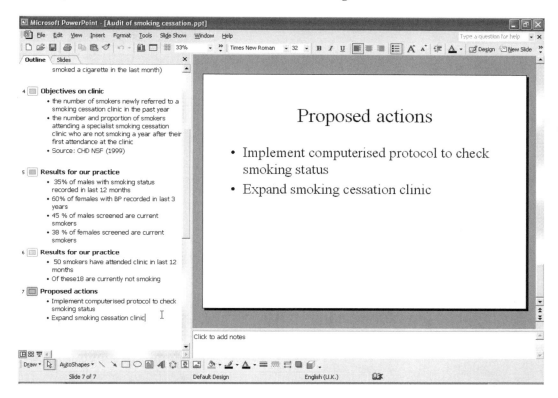

CD link
If you are still unsure, go to the CD and look in the Chapter 1 section. There you will find the completed presentation.

Now you can view your presentation. Either:

press [F5]

or

click on View
click on Show.

To move between the slides, either:

 press ↵

or

 press [PgDn].

At the end of the slide show, either:

✓◔ click to exit

or

 press [Esc].

Smart Alec says

'There is another way to view the presentation you're working on. That's to use the ▽ button at the bottom left-hand corner of the screen:

However, there is an important difference. The menu option and [F5] start the show at the beginning of the presentation. The ▽ icon starts with the slide you're working on.'

Now that you've finished your first presentation, you may want to save it or even print it.

To save it you may do one of three things:

✓◔ click on 🖫

or

✓◔ click on File
✓◔ click on Save

or

 press [Ctrl] and S.

Smart Alec says

'Well, I guess that you may be getting heartily sick of there always being three ways to do things! Just choose the one that works for you. There's often:

- a toolbar button: quick but often not offering any options
- a menu option: more flexible, but you have to remember where it is, and there are more clicks!
- a keyboard shortcut: quick but you have to remember them. Some are intuitive, e.g. [Ctrl]-F for Find, some are not, such as [Ctrl]-H for replace!'

Because there is no existing file name, the system will prompt you for one. If there is an existing file name, the system will use that unless you select the Save As option from the File menu (the shortcut for which is [F12]).

First, select a suitable folder for your presentation, then:

⌨ type 'Audit of smoking cessation'

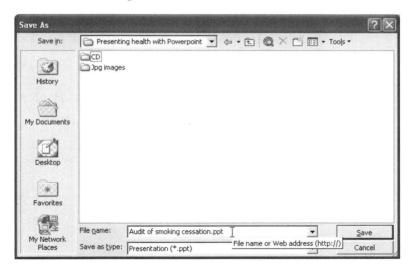

and either

⌨ press ↵

or

🖰 click on Save.

Note that the filename now appears in the title bar at the top of the screen.

You may quite reasonably want to print out your presentation. There are three common options.

- To print it out as slides, e.g. to copy onto acetates for OHPs.
- To print out handouts, which provide summaries of the presentation.
- To print out accompanying notes: but we've not done any of those yet, so we'll save that one!

To print out the presentation as slides:

   click on

and out should come seven pages, with one slide per page.

 **Smart Alec says**
'The printer icon actually prints out in one single step according to the current options you have set. As you haven't set any yet, it will print out the slides themselves. Like I said before, toolbar buttons are quick, but they're not flexible.'

If we want to change the printer options at all, e.g. to print out handouts, then we need to go to the printer dialog box. To do this:

   click on File
   click on Print (look for the keyboard shortcut for future reference).

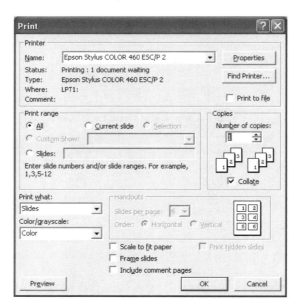

Here you can change the:

- printer
- print range (which slides you print)
- what you print (slides/handouts/notes)
- color or greyscale option (that's colour or black and white to you and me!).

To print out handouts:

- ⌐⌐ click on Slides in the Print what box
- ⌐⌐ change it so that Handouts is selected from the drop-down list.

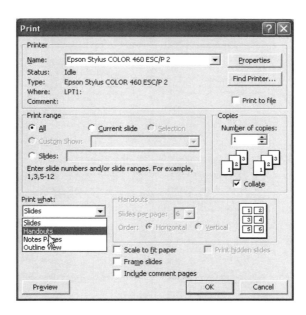

Once this step is completed, you can now access the handouts options and change the number and orientation of slides per page. Being a 'green' sort of chap, I'm going to stick with 6 per page to use my paper efficiently, but the 3 per page option is quite nice because it allows room for notes.

- ⌐⌐ Click on OK.

The results are shown below.

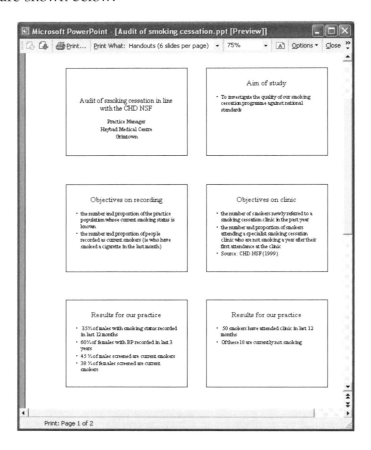

Over to you

See if you can print out handouts like this and also a set with 3 slides on a page.

Over to you

You will find an outline presentation below. Your task is to produce a PowerPoint presentation corresponding to it.

Smart Alec says

'For those of you unfamiliar with Windows, you'll need a new presentation. To open a new (blank) presentation:

click on 🗋.

And yes, before you ask, there is a keyboard shortcut and a menu option, but if you want it, you're going to have to find it!'

Chapter 1 of *Presenting Health with PowerPoint*

Learning outcomes

What the PowerPoint screen looks like

Screen layout
Menu structure
Toolbars

How to write an outline

How to add a heading
How to move to the next level
How to add the next slide

How to view the presentation

Use of the View menu
Use of the [F5] keyboard shortcut
Use of the 🖵 icon

Presentation management

How to create a new presentation
How to save a presentation
How to print a presentation

What you should know

At the end of each chapter, you will find a 'what you should know' section. In this chapter, I have presented it to you as the revision exercise above.

2

Making it more interesting

Beyond printed OHPs

By the end of the last chapter, we had a basic presentation and we'd seen how to turn it into a printed presentation. However, we can do a lot more with PowerPoint, especially if we're going to display our presentation using a data projector or LCD panel.

Display options	
Printed OHP acetates	Reliable. Always worth having as a backup. Modern inkjet printers can give good results even for colour OHPs. Ensure that you use the right type of acetates.
35mm slides	Traditional choice. If your hospital or local Trust has an in-house facility for preparing them, 35mm slides can give very good results, especially in colour.
LCD panel	These connect up to a computer and sit on top of a conventional OHP. They often suffer from a lack of brightness and as data projectors have become cheaper and lighter they have become less popular.
Data projector	These have become cheaper, lighter and more robust in recent years and are now the display of choice for most situations. However, Smart Alec has a few reservations . . .

Smart Alec says

'The problem with data projectors occurs if you are presenting as part of a programme. If you can prepare your presentation on the machine on which it will be displayed, then that's OK. If not, you need to establish the following facts.

- ☑ What version of PowerPoint is to be used?
- ☑ What resolution screen will be used?
- ☑ How many colours will be displayed?
- ☑ Will it fit on a floppy to move the file from my machine to the display machine?
- ☑ If not, can I transfer it to a CD-ROM?

Finally, three tips if you're going down this road:

- ☑ Use the embed fonts option if possible when saving the file. This will ensure that the presentation uses the right fonts to show your presentation correctly. But it will make the file bigger.
- ☑ If you have any doubts at all, print off a set of OHPs to take with you as backup.
- ☑ Always try it first in situ without the audience.'

Making it look prettier

Let's start with our title slide.

Audit of smoking cessation in line
with the CHD NSF

Practice Manager
Haybad Medical Centre
Grimtown

To change the appearance of a piece of text we first select it and then alter its appearance.

✓🖱 Click on the title.
✓🖱 Select the text 'Audit of smoking cessation in line with the CHD NSF'.

Now we can change the following characteristics:

- font size
- font colour
- font style
- text alignment.

We shall demonstrate this in two ways, first using the toolbar buttons and then using the menus, which give us even more control. With the text selected:

✓🖱 Click on the font size drop-down box.

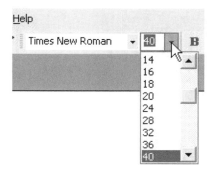

✓🖢 Click on 24.

Audit of smoking cessation in line with the CHD NSF

The text shrinks to 24pt, and fits on one line. Now repeat the process and select 54 from the drop-down box:

Audit of smoking cessation in line with the CHD NSF

We can also change the typeface or font itself.

✓🖢 Click on the font drop-down box.

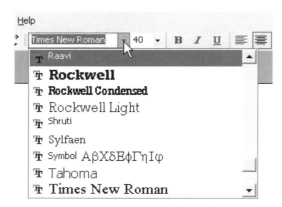

✓🖢 Select Arial from the list.

Audit of smoking cessation in line with the CHD NSF

Oops – Arial takes up more space. Try shrinking the font size back to 40!

🖮 Click on the font size drop-down box.

🖮 Click on 40.

Audit of smoking cessation in line with the CHD NSF

Smart Alec says
'In case you're worried, the text will appear black again as soon as we highlight something else!

From now on, we'll just show the text's final appearance, but remember; it needs to be highlighted first for the change to work!'

Next we can change the alignment and add bold, italic or underlining. Ensure the text is highlighted, then:

🖮 click on ≡ .

The alignment changes to left:

Audit of smoking cessation in line with the CHD NSF

🖮 Click on ≡ .

Audit of smoking cessation in line with the CHD NSF

🖮 Click on ≡ to revert to the original alignment.

Now we can add other effects.

🖮 Click on **B** .

Audit of smoking cessation in line with the CHD NSF

🖱 Click on *I* .

Audit of smoking cessation in line with the CHD NSF

🖱 Click on **B** again to remove the emboldening.

Audit of smoking cessation in line with the CHD NSF

🖱 Click on **U** to add an underline.

Audit of smoking cessation in line with the CHD NSF

🖱 Click on **U** to remove the underline.
🖱 Click on *I* to remove the italics.

Smart Alec says
'Try not to use underlining. In today's world it generally means that there is a hyperlink to another document and this may confuse the watcher. Use bold or italic for emphasis instead.'

For more detailed options, make sure the text is highlighted and then:

🖱 click on F̲ormat
🖱 click on F̲ont.

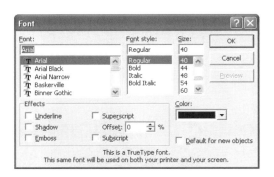

In addition to the options already accessed through the toolbar buttons, you can now add shadow effects or embossing or make text super- or subscript.

To add shadow:

☞ click on Shadow; a tick appears next to it

☞ click on OK.

Audit of smoking cessation in line with the CHD NSF

To look at some more features, let's move to the next but one slide.

⌨ Press [PgDn] twice.

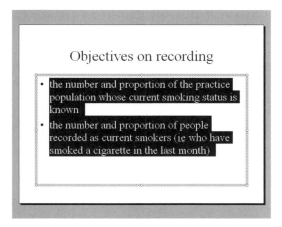

⌨ Click on the bullet points.

⌨ Select the text.

We can change the bullet character:

✓🖐 Click on Format.
✓🖐 Click on Bullets and numbering.
✓🖐 Select the tick bullet.

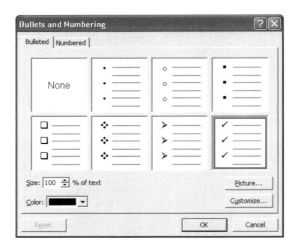

✓🖐 Click on OK.

The list now has tick bullets:

✓ the number and proportion of the practice
   population whose current smoking status is
   known
✓ the number and proportion of people recorded
   as current smokers (ie who have smoked a
   cigarette in the last month)

We can space the text differently as well:

✓🖐 Click on Format.
✓🖐 Click on Line spacing.

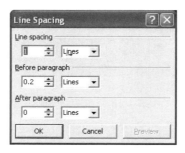

✍ Increase the line spacing to 0.3 Lines before and after.
✍ Click on OK.

> ✓ the number and proportion of the practice
> population whose current smoking status is
> known
>
> ✓ the number and proportion of people recorded as
> current smokers (ie who have smoked a cigarette
> in the last month)

Formatting for the whole presentation

All this stuff is very nice, but it can be a time-consuming business to adjust the format of each slide. Fortunately, you don't have to do this for every slide. You can do it once to the slide master. This has two advantages:

- it saves you a lot of effort
- it increases consistency and helps with establishing a house style (we will return to this in Chapter 4).

To access the slide master:

✍ click on View
✍ click on Master
✍ click on Slide Master.

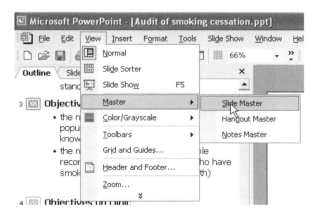

and the following screen appears:

Smart Alec says
'Changes made here apply to all slides.'

Smart Alec says

'I really hate that paper clip. If you do, then you can get rid of it:

🖰 right-click on the paper clip

🖰 select <u>H</u>ide

Ha!

   Actually, it's called the Office Assistant. If you find it helpful then you may at least like to turn it into a friendly pet:

🖰 right-click on the paper clip

🖰 select <u>C</u>hoose assistant

🖰 click on Next till you find Rocky or Links

🖰 click on OK.

If you delete the Office Assistant and want it back:

🖰 click on <u>H</u>elp

🖰 click on <u>S</u>how the office assistant.'

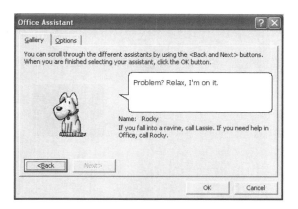

Let's change the background colour for our presentation.

Smart Alec says

'Watch out: he's colour-blind!'

The book's in black and white anyway, Alec!

'This book's not big enough for two smart alecs!'

To change the background colour:

- ◌ click on Format
- ◌ click on Background
- ◌ click on the drop-down list in the background fill box.

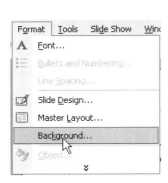
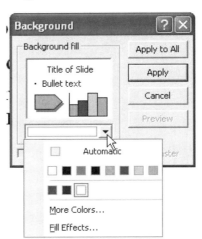

- ◌ Click on More colours.
- ◌ Choose a colour from the options available.

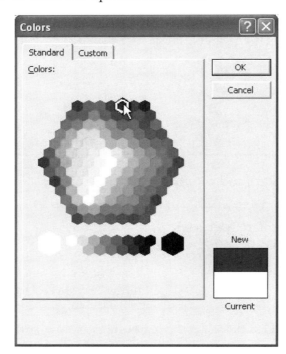

Click on OK.

 Click on Apply.

Smart Alec says

'Because you're applying the background to the master, all slides will show it. Thus in this case, it matters not if you click on Apply or Apply to All.'

You have now set a coloured background for your presentation.

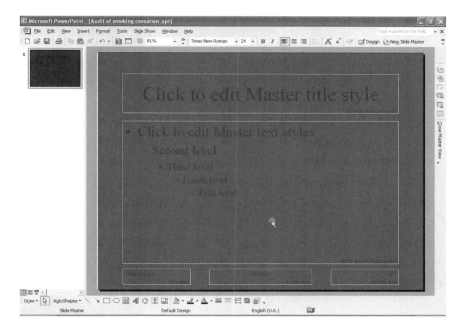

However, it is a flat colour and may be improved by adding gradient or texture.

✓🖑 Click on Format.
✓🖑 Click on Background.
✓🖑 Click on the drop-down list in the background fill box.
✓🖑 Click on Fill effects.
✓🖑 Select Diagonal up.

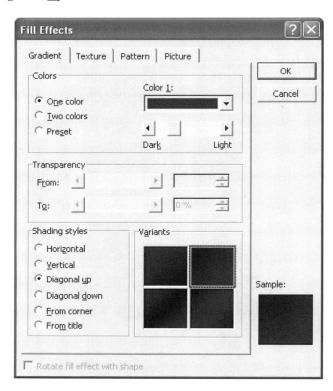

✓🖑 Click on OK.
✓🖑 Click on Apply.

This gives the background a graded look which may be more attractive than the flat look.

Over to you

Try some of the options we've been looking at. Try two colours instead of one and try the different styles of gradient. There are 24 different variants for each one colour alone.

But if this doesn't appeal we can use a texture instead. At the Fill Effects dialog box:

click on Texture.

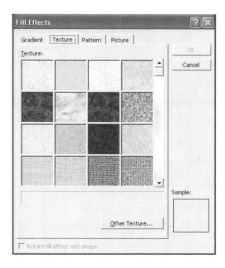

To choose a texture:

 click on the sample of your choice
 click on OK
 click on Apply.

I think that some of them are truly hideous. For example, 'denim':

Smart Alec says
'Thank goodness the book's in monochrome!'

But some of the subtler effects can be effective. You can also import your own textures. We'll look at this in Chapter 5.

Over to you
Please return the background to a graded dark blue colour.

Now we've got the background right, we can format the text for the entire presentation.

We're going to set up the following colour scheme:

Text	Font	Colour	Effect	Size
Master title style	Comic Sans MS	Light Blue	Shadow	40pt
Master text styles	Arial	Green	None	32pt
Master second level style	Arial	Green	None	24pt

You can do it in one of two ways: through the menus or by using the toolbar buttons.

Smart Alec says
'You've already seen all the toolbar buttons you need to use earlier in the chapter, except the one to change the colour of the text. Look for the **A ▾** icon if you want to use the toolbar buttons.'

We shall use the menus because they provide all the options in one place.

- ✍ Click on Click to edit Master title style.
- ✍ Click on Format.
- ✍ Click on Font.
- ✍ Select the options shown below.

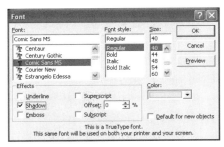

- ✍ Click on OK.
- ✍ Click on Click to edit Master text styles.
- ✍ Click on Format.
- ✍ Click on Font.
- ✍ Select the options show below.

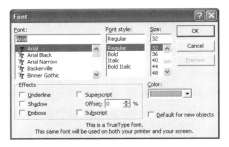

- ✍ Click on OK.
- ✍ Click on Click to edit Second level.
- ✍ Click on Format.
- ✍ Click on Font.
- ✍ Select the options show below.

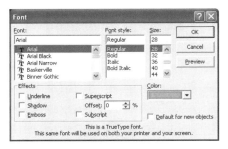

- ✍ Click on OK.

These properties are applied to all the slides in the presentation.

 Press [F5] to view the effect of your changes.

 **CD link**
If you are unsure, go to the CD and look in the Chapter 2 section. There you will find the completed presentation, listed as 'Audit based upon master'.

 Over to you
What sort of impression does this presentation now make?

- Is it formal or informal?
- Is it more impressive than it was in black and white?

We shall return to this in Part Two of this book.

Animation effects

Up till now, all the benefits of PowerPoint can be enjoyed by anybody with a £60 colour printer from Dixons and a box of blank OHP transparency slides. The next section will make our presentation dynamic and requires on-screen presentation, preferably via a data projector.

PowerPoint divides animations into 'preset' and 'custom'.

- Animation schemes (known as preset animations in versions prior to XP) are set by the system and are the easiest to use.
- Custom animations are a little more complicated to use, but give you more control.

 **Smart Alec says**
'Good presentations use effects according to the three 'S's:

- subtly
- sparingly
- sympathetically.'

We shall start with something very simple and apply the same scheme to all the slides.

To start, make sure that the screen is set to Normal view. If you're still in Master view:

- ✍ click on View
- ✍ click on Normal.

Once in Normal view:

- ✍ click on Slide show
- ✍ click on Animation Schemes.

Note that both side panels on the screen change to help you:

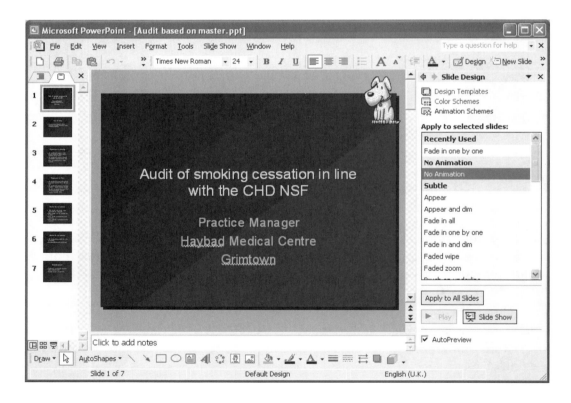

Heeding Alec's advice, we'll stick to the subtle section.

In the slide design panel on the right:

- ✍ click on Fade in one by one
- ✍ click on Apply to All Slides
- ✍ click on the Slide Show button to see the effect.

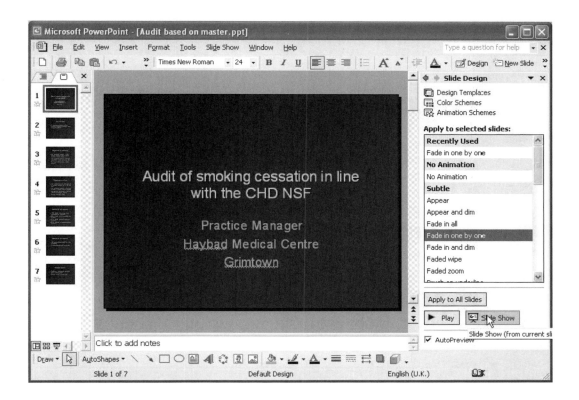

Smart Alec says
'Neat isn't it?
 Do remember that you still have to click the mouse to move on to each point in turn!'

Now suppose we want to add slide transitions:

- ✍ click on Slide show
- ✍ click on Slide Transition
- ✍ select Checkerboard Across
- ✍ click on Apply to All Slides
- ✍ click on the Slide Show button to see the effect.

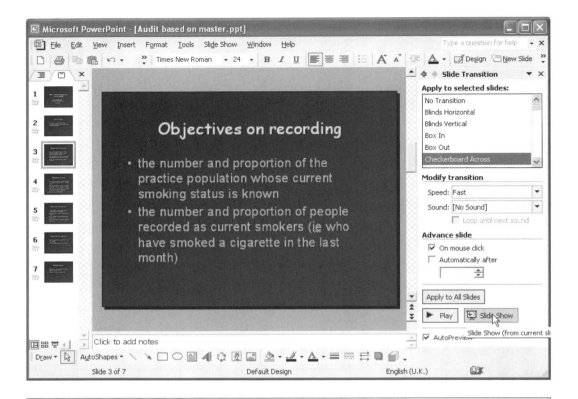

Over to you
It's showtime. Have a play. Have fun. Try some wacky transitions and effects. One of the best things about the XP version of PowerPoint is the greater choice of subtle effects.

However, sometimes we want to show different effects for different slides and tailor it to each slide. Before you do this, you may need to restore your presentation to the state it was in before you started to play!

✓☜ Select the title slide on the left-hand side of the screen (it's the one at the top!).

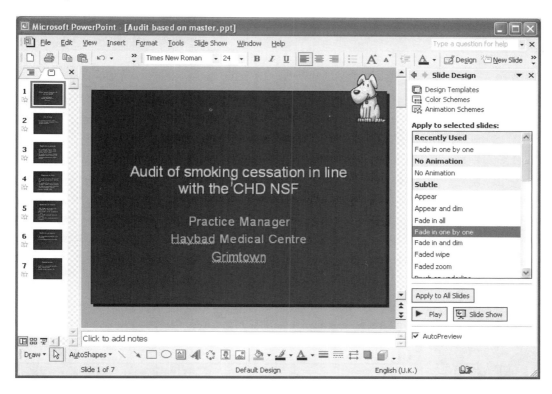

We want to bring all this text up on the screen at once, on this slide only.
   In the slide design panel on the right:

✓☜ click on Fade in one by one
✓☜ click on the Slide Show button to see the effect.

We can even tell it to move on without waiting for us!

✓☜ Click on Automatically after.
✓☜ Increase the time interval to 10 seconds.
✓☜ Click on the Slide Show button to see the effect.

Smart Alec says

'What you should observe is that after 10 seconds the next slide comes up automatically.

However, as we didn't remove the tick next to 'On mouse click', if you get impatient and click before the 10 seconds are up, then the next slide will appear anyway.'

However, sometimes you need to have even more control.

Consider, for example, the 'Objectives on recording' slide.

✓📖 Select slide 3 on the left-hand side of the screen.

We may want the first objective to disappear once we click for the next one.

To achieve this we must first remove the animation scheme.

✓📖 Click on Slide Show.

✓📖 Click on Animation Schemes.

✓📖 Click on No animation in the right-hand panel.

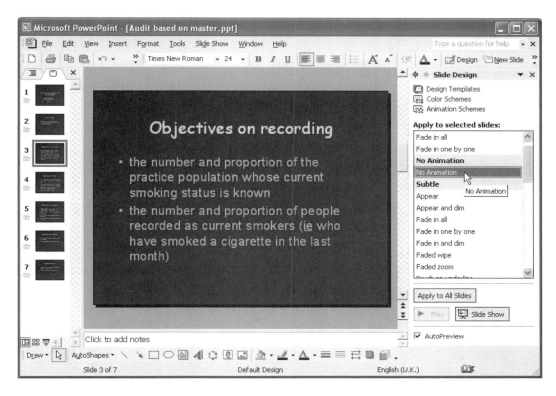

Next we have to add our custom animation.

✍🏻 Select the first bullet point.

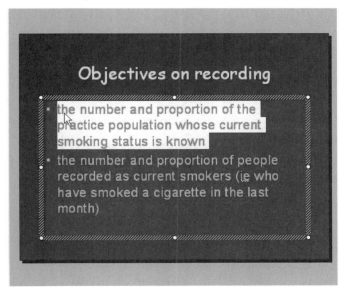

🖱 Click on Sli<u>d</u>e Show.

🖱 Click on Cus<u>to</u>m Animation.

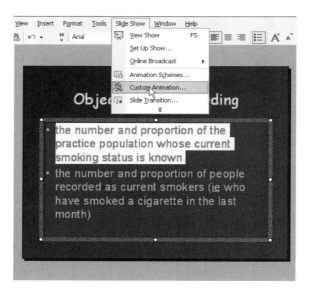

🖱 Click on Add Effect.

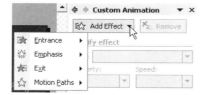

🖱 Click on <u>E</u>ntrance.

🖱 Select <u>5</u>. Fade from the resulting list.

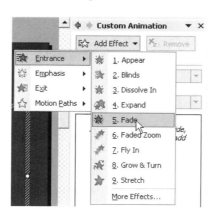

🖑 Click on Exit.

🖑 Select 5. Disappear from the resulting list.

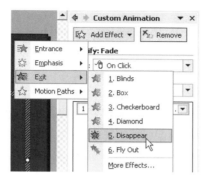

Now we'll animate the second bullet point.

🖑 Select the text associated with the second bullet point.

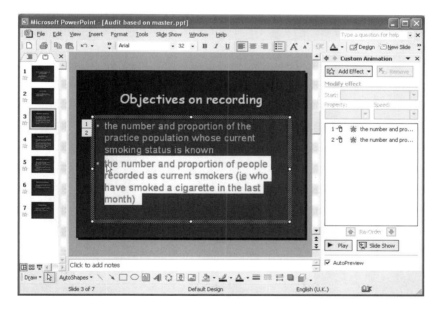

Smart Alec says

'If you look at the right-hand panel you'll see that you're building up a list of the transitions on this slide.'

🖑 Click on <u>E</u>ntrance.

🖑 Select <u>5</u>. Fade from the resulting list.

Now we tell it to start fading in the new bullet as soon as the previous bullet starts to disappear, otherwise it will wait for another mouse click.

🖑 Click on On Click in the Start drop-down box.

🖑 Select With Previous from the resulting list of options.

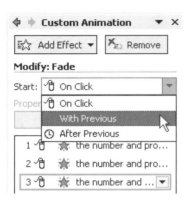

Now it's ready.

🖑 Click on the Slide Show button to see the effect.

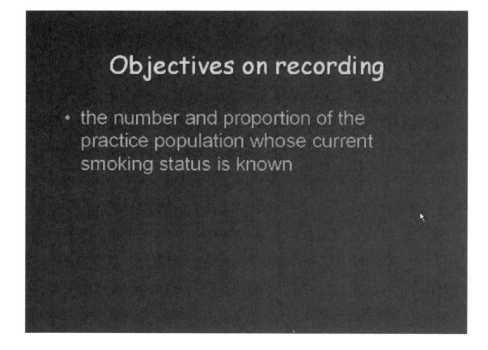

And then when you click again:

Objectives on recording

- the number and proportion of people recorded as current smokers (ie who have smoked a cigarette in the last month)

Over to you
It's showtime again. You've done a lot since your last play time. Have a play. Have fun. Try to reproduce the above custom animation on later slides.

Smart Alec says
'If you really want to be clever, try leaving the bullet points on the screen and changing the colour as the mouse is clicked.

Here are some hints as to how you might do it:

1 remove the animation scheme for all slides
2 use the Fade in all scheme for the first two slides
3 use the custom animation scheme for slides 3 to 7
4 apart from the slide with 4 bullets, each of the others needs the same animation.
5 start with the first bullet in yellow text
6 set it to change to green on click
7 set the second bullet to change to yellow using the With Previous option.'

CD link
Check out Alec's solution on the CD. You may also find the next two screenshots I snaffled from him helpful.

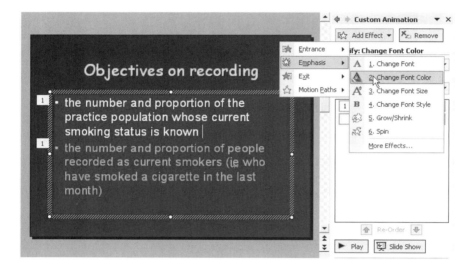

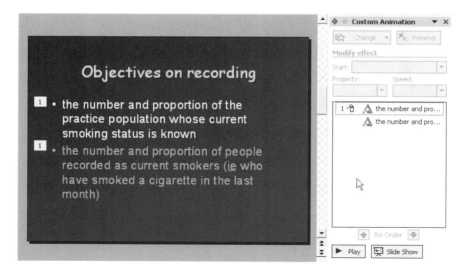

What you should know

The pros and cons of:

- using OHPs
- using 35mm slides
- using an LCD projection panel
- using a data projector.

How to format a slide:

- how to change font type
- how to apply italics, bold, underlining and case changes to text
- how to apply shadow to text, use sub-script and superscript
- how to apply different colours to text font
- how to centre text and align text left and right, top and bottom
- how to adjust line spacing
- how to change the type of bullets/numbers in a list.

How to use a whole presentation:

- how to use a master slide
- how to add a background.

How to use preset animation:

- how to add preset animation effects to slides
- how to change preset animation effects.

How to use custom animation effects:

- how to entrance effects
- how to exit effects.

How to use slide transition effects.

Smart Alec says
'Phew, there's a lot here! If you're not sure then have another go. Even I had to revise some of it, but don't tell him, because he thinks I'm really smart!'

3

Adding graphics, tables, charts, audio and video

A new scenario

So far we have looked only at text, and ignored the possibilities of using graphics, audio and video. In this chapter we will introduce these elements. In order to do this, we shall use a new scenario.

You are asked to produce a presentation to inform patients about the practice. The bare bones of the presentation can be found on the CD, or it can be constructed from the outline below.

CD link
The outline is available on the CD in the Chapter 3 section. The file is called 'Pristine practice outline.ppt'.

Smart Alec says
'Because you can't write to a CD-ROM, you will need to save a copy of the presentation onto your hard disk.

If the computer won't let you save the presentation to the same name, then make sure that the file properties are not set to Read-only.'

Pristine practice

- Upmarket health centre
- Snobbytown

Our practice

- 8,000 patients
- 4 full time GPs, plus 1 part time
- 2 practice nurses
- Practice manager
- 4 reception staff
- Purpose built premises

The GPs

- Dr Smith
- Dr Smith
- Dr Jones
- Dr Boatman
- Dr Singh

Patient services

- Well women clinic
- Well men clinic
- Healthy heart clinic
- Stop smoking clinic

Smoking reduction

	Status recorded		Smoking rates	
	Men	Women	Men	Women
1999	30%	45%	40%	35%
2000	40%	60%	42%	33%
2001	48%	72%	39%	30%

Patients offered appointment same day

- 1999: 56%
- 2000: 45%
- 2001: 48%

Patients missing appointments

- 1999: 3.2%
- 2000: 3.8%
- 2001: 4.5%

Action plans for 2002

- Continued action on smoking
- Patient awareness re missed appointments
- Computerised blood pressure screening protocol
- Telemedicine pilot on dermatology

This outline contains the basic information we want to convey, but is frankly a little dull.

The first task is to add a coloured background to the slide master. Once you have the basic outline, switch to slide master view:

Click on <u>V</u>iew.

Click on <u>M</u>aster.

Click on <u>S</u>lide Master.

Over to you
The first task is a re-inforcement of the work carried out in the last chapter.

Element	Font	Colour	Effect	Size
Background	n/a	Light turquoise	Vertical shading	n/a
Master title style	Impact	Light blue	Shadow	44pt
Master text styles	Tahoma	Yellow	None	32pt
Master second level style	Tahoma	Yellow	None	24pt

It should look something like the following:

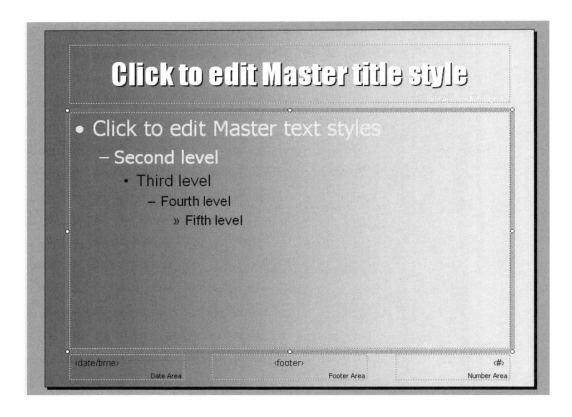

A useful thing to add to a master slide is a logo.

CD link
On the CD you will find a sample logo:

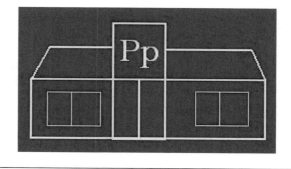

Smart Alec says
'Awful, isn't it? Still, what do you expect from Pristine Practice of Snobbytown?'

To add the logo to the slide master:

- click on Insert
- click on Picture.

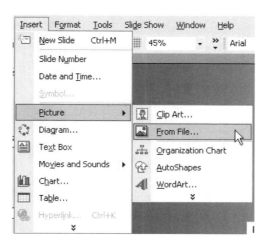

📖 Click on From File . . .

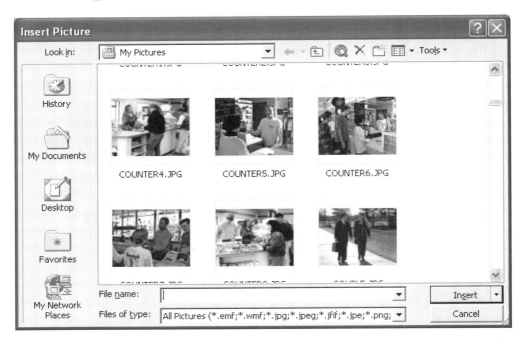

You will need to select the CD from the Look in drop-down list:

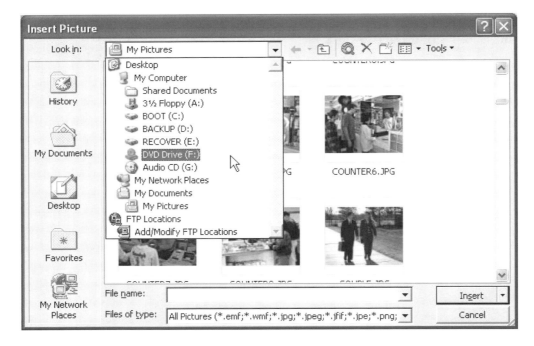

And then look in the Chapter 3 folder:

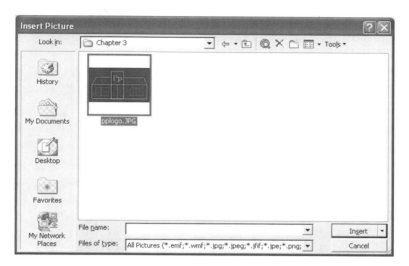

✎ Click on Insert.

✎ Drag the logo down to the bottom right-hand corner of the slide.

Now we will return to the individual slides.

⌐🖰 Click on View.
⌐🖰 Click on Normal.

The logo appears on each slide:

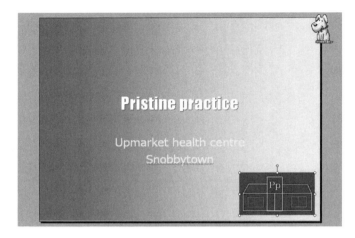

As this is the title slide, we might like to add a picture to liven it up. We can search Clip Art for a suitable image.

⌐🖰 Click on Insert.
⌐🖰 Click on Picture.
⌐🖰 Click on Clip Art.

The Insert Clip Art panel appears at the right-hand side of the screen. As we want an image appropriate for a medical context, we'll ask for an image related to 'doctor'.

Type 'doctor' in the search text box.

Click on Search.

The system provides any relevant images.

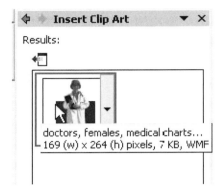

Smart Alec says
'The actual images will depend upon the Clip Art installed on your machine. You may well have a choice of options – unlike us!'

✓🗋 Click on the button next to the image to reveal a menu of options.
✓🗋 Click on Insert.

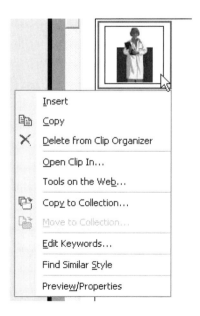

The image appears in the centre of the slide.

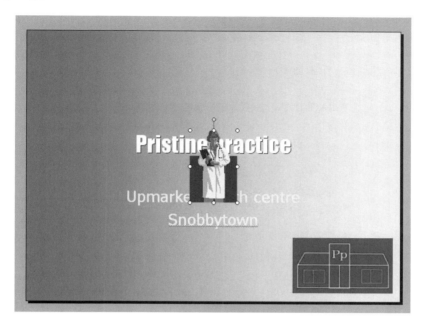

Next we shall:

🖱 drag the image down to the bottom left-hand corner
🖱 resize the image.

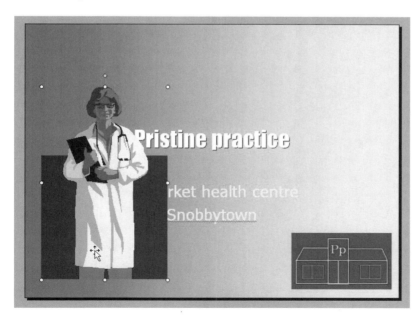

Unfortunately, the image sits on top of the text, so we will send it to the back of the slide so that the text can be seen.

✓ Click on Draw.
✓ Click on Order.
✓ Click on Send to Back.

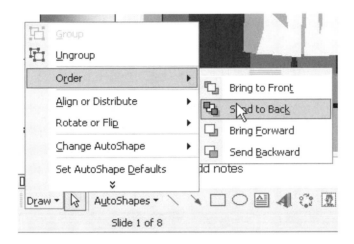

The result is that the image now appears *behind* the text.

Smart Alec says
'Each slide is made up of a series of objects lying on top of each other in a series of layers:

If we use the Send Backward option, the selected option moves down one layer:

If we use Send to Back, it goes to the bottom of the pile:'

Press [PgDn] to move to the next slide.
Press [PgDn] again to move to the GPs slide.

Organisational charts

We can present this information as an organisational chart:

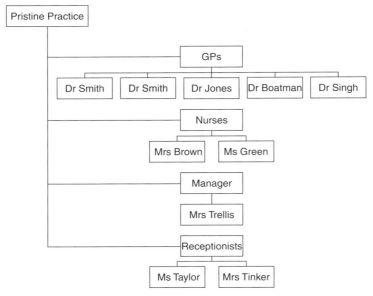

To add an organisational chart to our presentation, we will edit the existing slide.

🖱 Select the word 'GPs'.
⌨ Overtype 'Practice'.
🖱 Select the main text area.
⌨ Press [Del] to delete the text box.

The slide should now look like this:

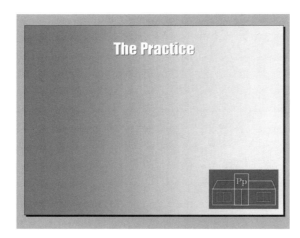

🗅 Click on <u>I</u>nsert.
🗅 Click on Diag<u>r</u>am.
🗅 Click on the organisational chart icon:

🗅 Click on OK.

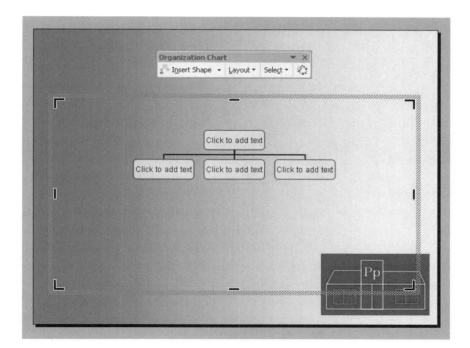

🗅 Click on the top box.
⌨ Type 'Pristine Practice'.
🗅 Click on the left-hand box in the next row.
⌨ Type 'GPs'.
🗅 Click on the next box.

▨ Type 'Nurses'.
✓🖮 Click on the next box.
▨ Type 'Manager'.

In the toolbox, click on Insert shape.

✓🖮 Click on Co-worker to add another box in the same tier.
✓🖮 Click on the new box.
▨ Type 'Receptionists'.

This completes the first tier.

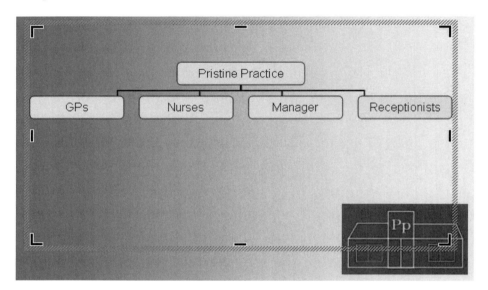

To add the next row:

✓🖮 click on GPs.

In the toolbox, click on Insert shape.

✓🖮 Click on Subordinate to add a box in the next tier.
✓🖮 Click on the new box.
▨ Type 'Dr Smith'.

In the toolbox, click on Insert shape.

✓🖮 Click on Co-worker to add another box in the same tier.
▨ Type 'Dr Smith'.

In the toolbox, click on Insert shape.

✓🖮 Click on Co-worker to add another box in the same tier.
▨ Type 'Dr Jones'.

In the toolbox, click on Insert shape.

 Click on Co-worker to add another box in the same tier.

Type 'Dr Boatman'.

In the toolbox, click on Insert shape.

 Click on Co-worker to add another box in the same tier.

Type 'Dr Singh'.

This completes the GPs.

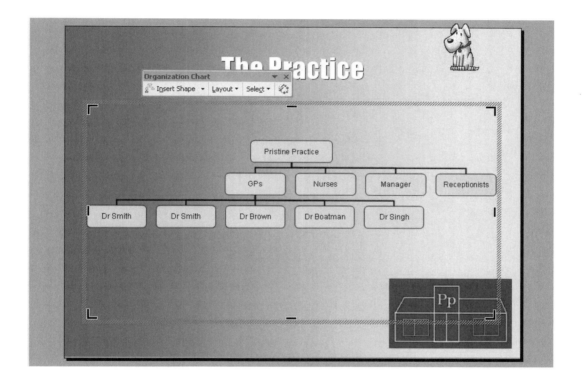

Over to you

Add the following staff to the structure:

Nurses: Mrs Brown, Ms Green
Manager: Mrs Trellis
Receptionists: Ms Taylor, Mrs Tinker.

The end result is practically unreadable, with fonts shrunk to a ridiculous 3 point!

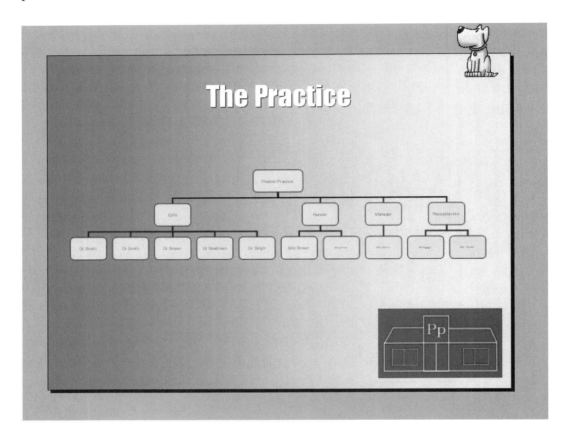

One solution is to change the layout to a vertical arrangement, which fits better on the slide.

To change the chart to a vertical arrangement:

- select Pristine Practice
- on the chart toolbar, select the Layout drop-down list
- select Right Hanging.

This still leaves the text illegible. To increase the font size:

- select the entire chart by dragging the mouse over the entire chart
- select 11pt from the top tool bar as the font size.

The result is a little better.

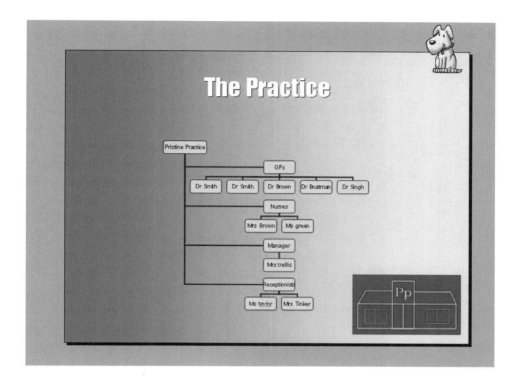

Smart Alec says
'Organisational charts can be a really good way to ruin a presentation if handled badly. Have a look in Part Two to find out more.'

Inserting a table

The next but one slide contains data that would be better in a table. Move forward to the Smoking reduction slide.

⌨ Press [PgDn] to move to the next slide.

⌨ Press [PgDn] again to move to the Smoking reduction slide.

The data may be represented as a table:

	Status recorded		Smoking rates	
	Men	Women	Men	Women
1999	30%	45%	40%	35%
2000	40%	60%	42%	33%
2001	48%	72%	39%	30%

To insert a table like this onto the slide, first delete the bulleted text and its associated text frame.

 Select the bulleted text.
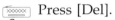 Press [Del].
 Select the text frame.
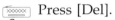 Press [Del].

Now we can add the table.

 Click on Insert.
 Click on Table.

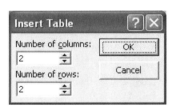

 Increase Number of columns to 5.
 Increase Number of rows to 5.
 Click on OK.

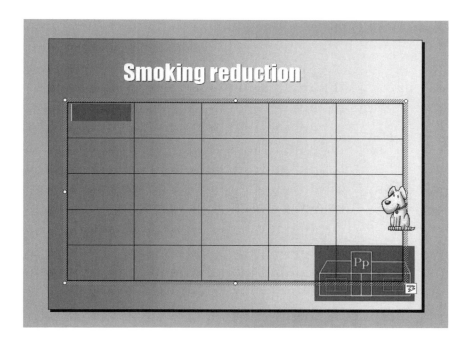

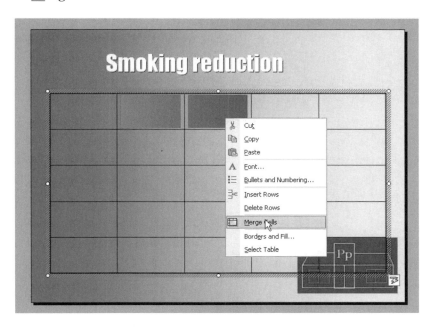

Press [Tab] to move to the next cell.

Select this cell and the one next to it.

Right-click on the highlighted cells.

Select Merge Cells.

The two cells are merged.

- Type 'Status recorded'.
- Press [Tab] to move to the next cell.
- Select this cell and the one next to it.
- Right-click on the highlighted cells.
- Select Merge Cells.
- Type 'Smoking rates'.

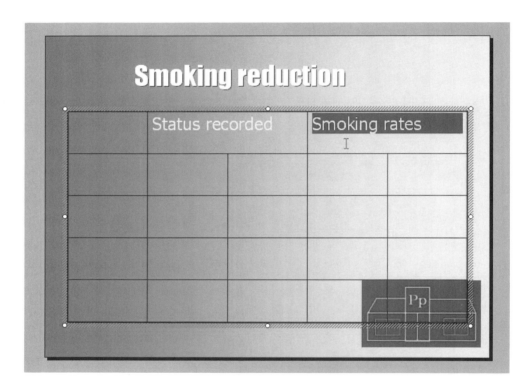

- Press [Tab] to move to the next row.
- Press [Tab] to move to the next cell.
- Type 'Men'.
- Press [Tab] to move to the next cell.
- Type 'Women'.
- Press [Tab] to move to the next cell.
- Type 'Men'.
- Press [Tab] to move to the next cell.
- Type 'Women'.
- Select the first two rows of cells.
- Click on ≡ to centre align the text.

Before . . . left aligned:

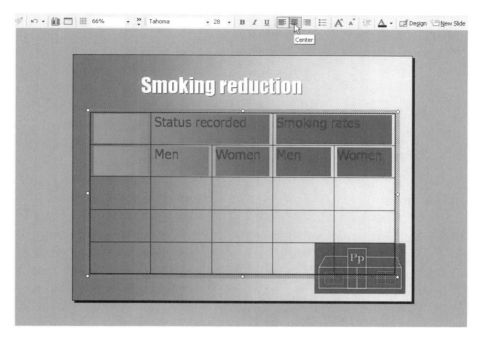

After . . . centre aligned:

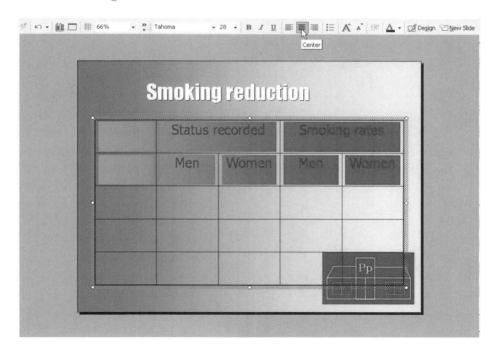

Over to you
Completing the rest of the table uses the same functions as above. See if you can do it. Note that the years are left aligned whilst the rest of the cells are centre aligned.

To help you, there's one I prepared earlier shown below!

Smoking reduction

	Status recorded		Smoking rates	
	Men	Women	Men	Women
1999	30%	45%	40%	35%
2000	40%	60%	42%	33%
2001	48%	72%	39%	30%

Smart Alec says
Ugh! The table overlaps the logo. Can't you do anything about it?

Alright, Alec, just for you . . .

To hide the logo we'll give the table a background colour.

- ✓🖰 Select all the cells in the table.
- ✓🖰 Right-click on the table.

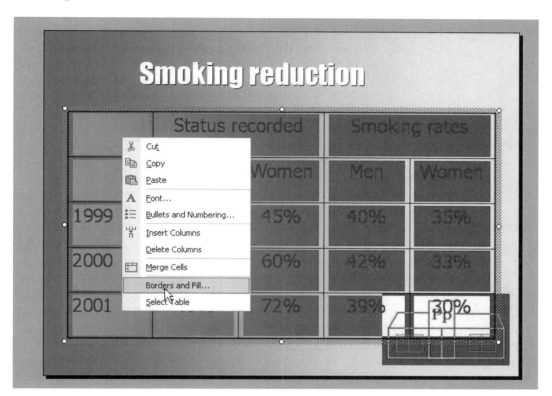

- ✓🖰 Select Borders and Fill.

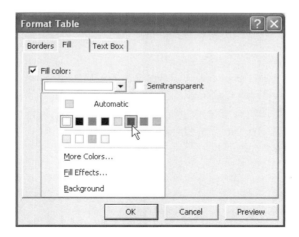

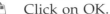 Select a dark blue background.
 Click on OK.

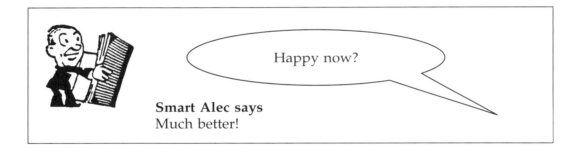

Smart Alec says
Much better!

Alternatively, if you already have the table in a Word document, you can copy and paste it in. To demonstrate this, first delete your table from the slide:

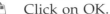 select the table
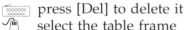 press [Del] to delete it
 select the table frame

CD link
On the CD you will find a file called 'Sample table.doc' in the Chapter 3 folder.

press [Del] to delete it.

Open the file in Word.

Select the table.

Click on 🖹.

Close Word.

With the PowerPoint slide open on the screen:

click on 📋.

The table appears on the screen:

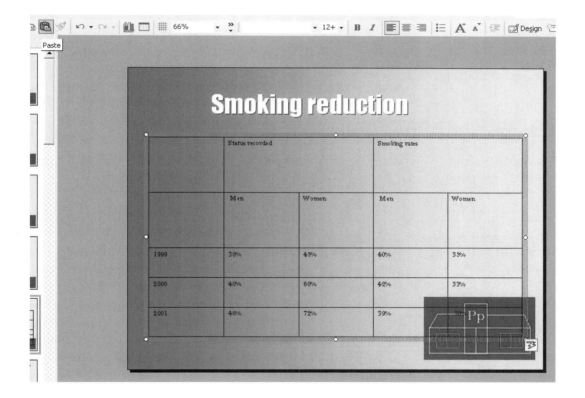

Over to you

Formatting the table uses the same functions as above. See if you can do it. Note that the font used earlier is 26pt Tahoma in yellow. If you need help with font formatting, refer back to the previous chapter.

This has the advantage of preventing typing errors, but it still needs formatting.

Smart Alec says
'You can copy and paste almost anything onto a Power-Point slide. To the computer they are all just objects, so if you can copy it, you can put it onto a PowerPoint slide. This includes:

• pictures
• organisational charts
• graphs

and is particularly useful if you have a Word version of a report or an Excel spreadsheet with pretty graphs in it.'

Introducing graphs

The easiest way to introduce a graph is to produce it in Excel and copy and paste it into PowerPoint. If you have Excel, then try the following exercise:

CD link
On the CD you will find a file called 'Sample chart.xls' in the Chapter 3 folder.

 Open the file in Excel.
 Select the worksheet labelled Chart1.

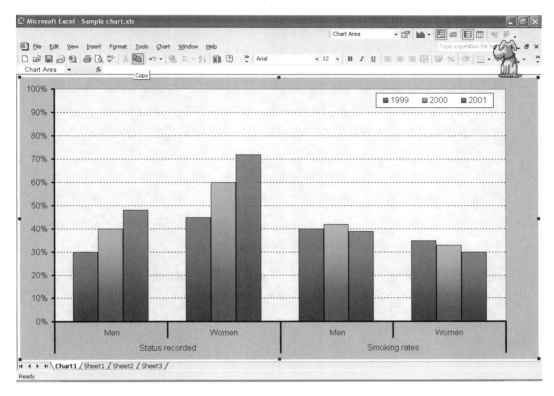

⤷ Click on ⬚ .
⤷ Close Excel.

Return to PowerPoint.

To replace your table with a chart, delete your table from the slide:

⤷ select the table
⌨ press [Del] to delete it
⤷ select the table frame
⌨ press [Del] to delete it

and then

⤷ click on ⬚ .

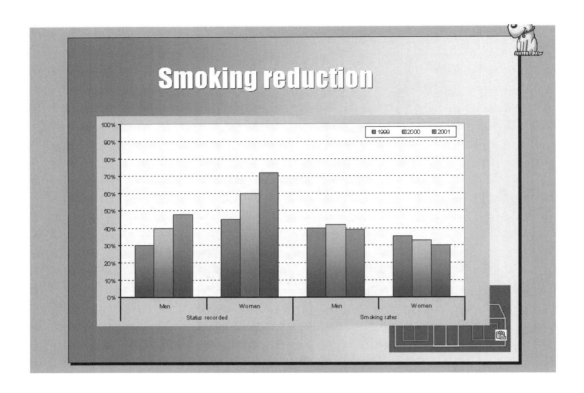

Smart Alec says
'For those of you without Excel, you can copy and paste the same chart from the Paint application, by opening the file 'sample chart.jpg' in the Paint application, and then going through the same delete the table, copy and paste process. I sneaked it on the CD when he wasn't looking!'

CD link
On the CD you will find a file called 'Sample chart.jpg' in the Chapter 3 folder.

The alternative strategy – drawing the graph within PowerPoint – is frankly horrible and should be avoided at all costs. However, for the masochists amongst you . . .

Smart Alec says
'Miss this bit out if you have a copy of *Excel in Clinical Governance* . . . go to the next section heading. Honestly, trust me!'

To replace your table with a chart drawn in PowerPoint, delete your existing table or chart from the slide:

 select the table or chart
 press [Del] to delete it
 select the table frame
 press [Del] to delete it
 click on Insert
 click on Chart.

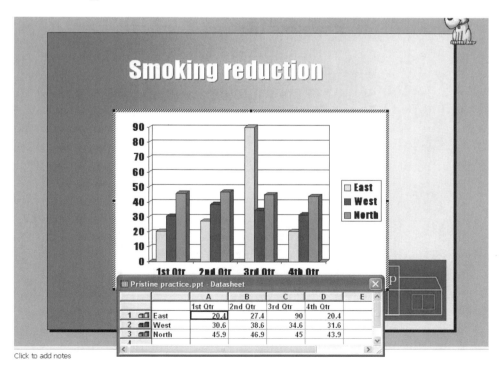

✓📖 Open the file on the CD in the Chapter 3 folder called 'Sample table.doc'.
✓📖 Select the table.
✓📖 Click on 📋.
✓📖 Close Word.

Return to PowerPoint.

✓📖 Click on the top left-hand cell in the Datasheet window:

		A	B	C	D	E
		1st Qtr	2nd Qtr	3rd Qtr	4th Qtr	
1	East	20.4	27.4	90	20.4	
2	West	30.6	38.6	34.6	31.6	
3	North	45.9	46.9	45	43.9	

Pristine practice.ppt - Datasheet

✓📖 Click on 📋.

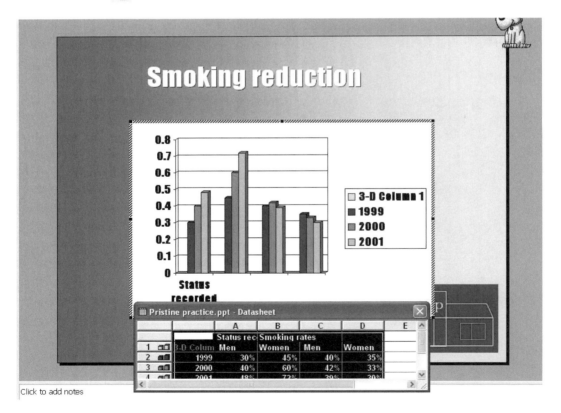

To make this chart more respectable:

✓📖 right-click on the chart.

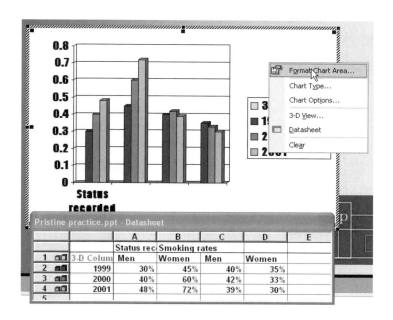

		A	B	C	D	E
		Status rec	Smoking rates			
1	3-D Colum	Men	Women	Men	Women	
2	1999	30%	45%	40%	35%	
3	2000	40%	60%	42%	33%	
4	2001	48%	72%	39%	30%	
5						

Over to you

I'm not going to encourage you any further in this madness. However, if you like a challenge, try to emulate the solution I produced, shown below.

To do this, I cheated by deleting the first row and adding the top row labels manually as the axis title. Otherwise, it's quite like Excel, just harder work. Trust me, I'm a PhD!

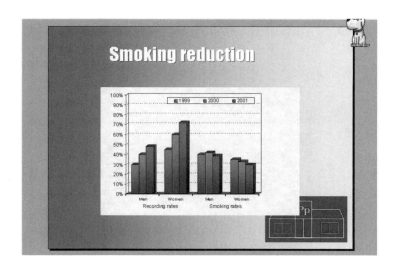

Adding photos to your presentation

The actual process of adding a photograph to your presentation is the same as adding a line drawing, the same process we used to add a logo to our master slide, or the image on the title slide.

We shall illustrate this by replacing the rather cheesy Clip Art on the title slide with a tasteful black and white photograph of the health centre.

- Press [Ctrl] and [Home] together to return to the title slide.
- Select the Clip Art illustration.
- Press [Del] to remove it.
- Click on the 'Pristine Practice' text.
- Drag it up to clear a blank area in the middle of the slide.
- Click on the remaining text.
- Drag it down to clear a blank area in the middle of the slide.

CD link
On the CD you will find a photo called 'photo1.jpg' in the Chapter 3 folder.

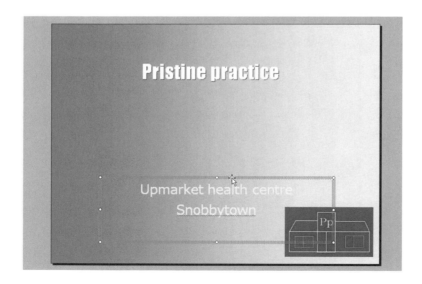

- ✓🕮 Click on Insert.
- ✓🕮 Click on Picture.
- ✓🕮 Select From File.
- ✓🕮 Select the Chapter 3 folder on the CD as the folder.
- ✓🕮 Select photo1.jpg as the image.

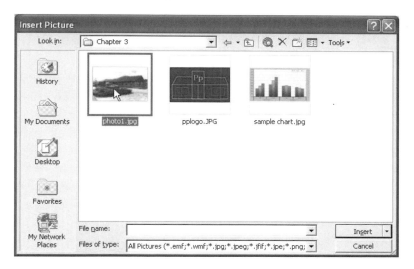

- ✓🕮 Select Insert.

You may need to re-arrange the text and image a little to achieve the correct result:

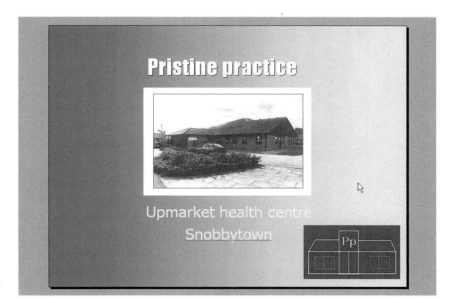

You can add a shadow effect to the photograph. These features are accessible through the toolbar button at the right-hand end of the drawing toolbar, usually at the bottom of the screen:

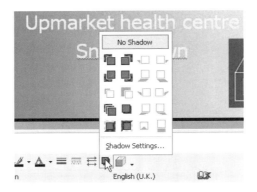

To apply a shadow effect:

- click on the photograph to select it
- click on the shadow button
- select Shadow Style 5 from the options:

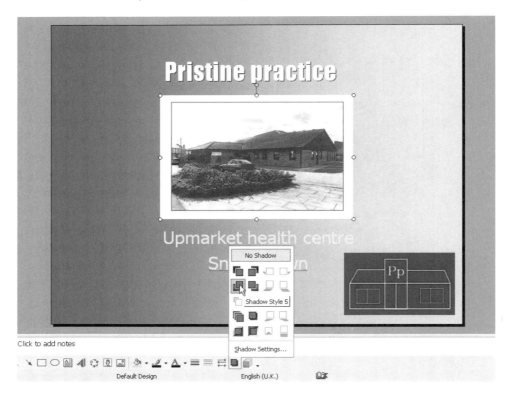

And the result looks like this:

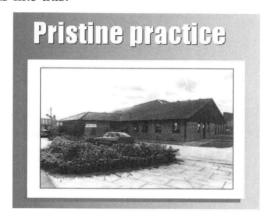

Smart Alec says
'There are a number of different ways in which you can produce your own digitised photos for your presentations. See the table below for some ideas. You don't need a digital camera or scanner. Boots or any other photography shop can produce a CD of digitised photos from a 35mm film, so don't throw away the Leica just yet!'

Method	Advantages	Disadvantages
Digital camera	Convenience Instant results No processing costs Can be very compact Can be added straight from the Insert/Picture option in PowerPoint	Low resolution Connecting camera to PC involves installing software
Scanned photographs	Very high quality Can use existing photos Can be done in-house Can be added straight from the Insert/Picture option in PowerPoint	Needs a scanner! Connecting scanner to PC involves installing software
CD-ROM produced by photo lab from 35mm film	Very high quality Uses existing equipment	Cost Delay Can't be done in-house

Adding lines, boxes and text boxes to your presentation

We will use the last slide to illustrate the use of boxes, lines and text boxes to add emphasis to a slide.

⌨ Press [Ctrl] and [End] together to move to the last slide.
🖱 Click on the Line button on the drawing toolbar:

🖱 Click on the point where you want the line to start.
🖱 Drag the pointer to the place you want the line to end.

🖱 And let go.

To make the line thicker:

🖱 select the line thickness toolbar button on the drawing toolbar
🖱 select 4½ pt as the line thickness.

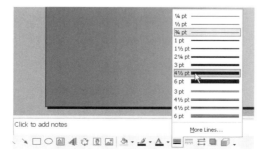

The result looks like this:

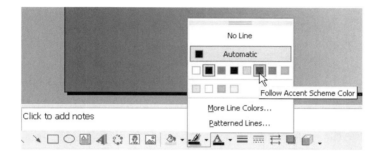

We can change the colour using the line colour toolbar button.

✓🖑 Click on the Line colour toolbar button.
✓🖑 Select dark blue from the resulting menu.

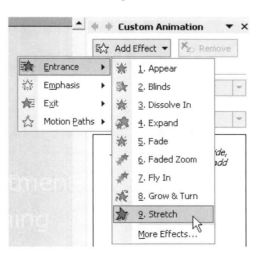

To add further emphasis we can add an entrance effect.

✓🖑 Click on Slide Show.
✓🖑 Click on Custom Animation.
✓🖑 Click on Add Effect.
✓🖑 Click on Entrance.
✓🖑 Select 9. Stretch from the resulting list.

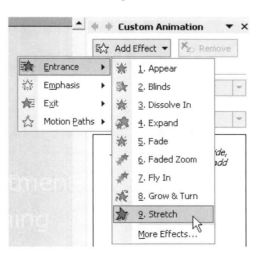

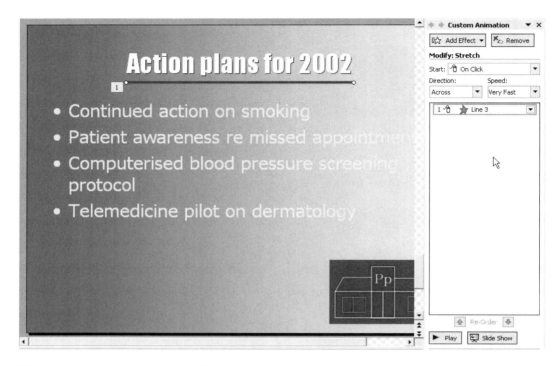

From the Start: drop-down list

✓🖑   select After Previous.

To see the effect:

✓🖑   click on Slide Show.

Now, to finish off the presentation we'll add a new slide.

✓🖑   Click on Insert.
✓🖑   Click on New Slide.

In the panel at the right-hand side:

🖝 select a blank layout.

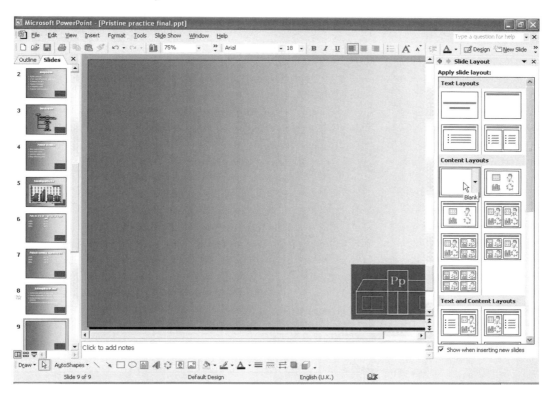

Now we'll add a text box.

🖝 Click on the text box button.

⌨ Type 'The End'.

🖱 Right-click on the text.

🖱 Select Format Text Box from the resulting menu:

🖱 Click on the Fill Colour drop-down list.

🖱 Select a dark blue background for the text box.

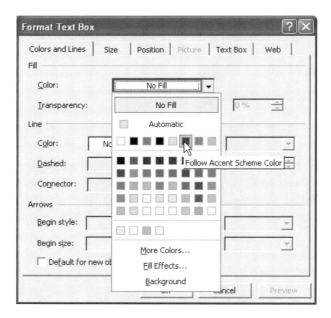

🖱 Click on OK.

The text is a bit small. To enlarge the text, go to the font size drop-down list and
select 96 as the point size.

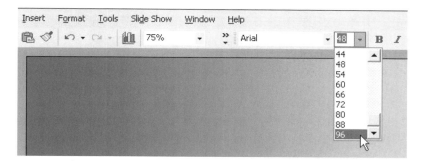

To further emphasise the message we can make the box 3-D.

- Click on the 3-D toolbar button in the drawing toolbar.
- Select the first option.

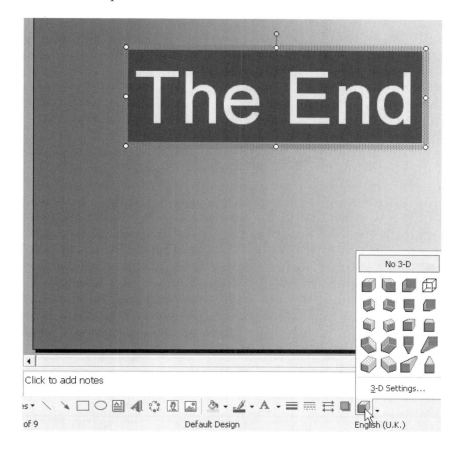

Over to you
You could improve this further by adding an entrance effect, similar to that used in the previous slide. As this is something you've done twice already, it's over to you!

Sound and video

You can add sound and vision in just the same way as any other object. However, be warned – they can be really cheesy! For example, let's add a round of applause at the end of our presentation.

🖑 Click on Insert.
🖑 Click on Movies and Sounds.
🖑 Click on Sound from Clip Organizer.

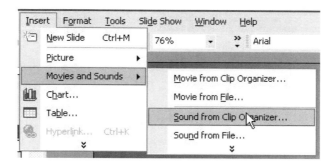

The available sound clips appear on the right-hand side of the screen. There should be one called 'applause.wav'.

🖑 Click on applause.wav.

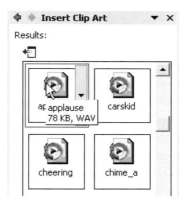

The Office Assistant (remember Rocky?) will ask if you want it to play automatically:

🖑 Click on Yes.

Smart Alec says
'I hate that silly speaker icon. If you do too, then shrink it till it's much smaller and drag it down to the bottom left-hand corner: it'll still work and it'll be out of the way!'

Over to you
If you added an entrance effect to the text box, then you may like to play with the animations so that the applause comes after the transition. As this is something you've done already, it's over to you!

In the same manner, you can add a range of audio and video clips.

Smart Alec says

'If you're going to use video, just make sure that your replay hardware is up to it. Video comes in huge files and needs lots of memory and disk space. Generally, if you want to go down this road it's best to consult a specialist technician, or at least a smart alec like me!'

Finishing touches

Over to you

There are more refinements you can make. In particular, slides 6 and 7 are crying out for some attention. For revision, make slide 6 into a table and slide 7 into a chart.

CD link

On the CD you will find a model answer presentation called 'Pristine Practice final.ppt' in the Chapter 3 folder.

What you should know

How to add graphics and images.

- How to add a piece of Clip Art.
- How to add an image using the Insert picture option.
- How to use Copy and Paste to add an image to a presentation.
- How to use the Cut and Paste tools to move an image within a presentation.
- How to delete an image.
- How to add lines and boxes:
  - how to draw a line
  - how to move lines in a slide

- how to change line colour/modify line width
- how to add various forms of shape – boxes, circles, etc. – to a slide
- how to rotate or flip a drawn object in a slide
- how to change the attributes of the shape; colour in the shape, change the line type
- how to apply shadow to a shape
- how to re-order the layers of a drawing.
- How to modify text boxes:
  - how to re-size and move text box within a slide
  - how to set line weights, style and colours of a text box.
- How to add charts and tables:
  - how to create an organisational chart
  - how to modify the structure of an organisational chart
  - how to create different kinds of charts; bar chart, pie chart, etc.
  - how to add a table.
- How to add images, sound and video:
  - how to import images from other files
  - how to resize and move an image in a slide
  - how to import other objects – text, spreadsheet, table, chart or graphic files – into a slide
  - how to copy an imported object to a master slide
  - how to add border effects to an object
  - how to add sound to a slide
  - how to add video.
- How to move around a presentation quickly:
  - how to move to the first slide
  - how to move to the last slide.

Smart Alec says
'If you're not sure about any of this, go back and try again. It's OK – nobody's looking!'

4

Setting up a house style

What is a house style?

We live in a world dominated by brands. Young children recognise multinational brands such as McDonalds before they know their alphabet. A house style is your chance to establish an identity for yourself, your project or organisation.

The house style determines the 'look and feel' of your presentation and includes the following elements:

- slide layout
- slide background
- font size and colour
- bullet characters
- logos.

PowerPoint has a range of features designed to help you implement your chosen style in a consistent fashion, many of which you have already met.

How to set up a house style

Return to the outline of the Pristine Practice presentation.

CD link
The outline is on the CD, in the Chapter 3 folder, stored as Pristine practice outline.ppt. There is also a shortcut to the outline in the Chapter 4 folder, so:

🖱 click on the 'Shortcut to Pristine practice outline.ppt'.

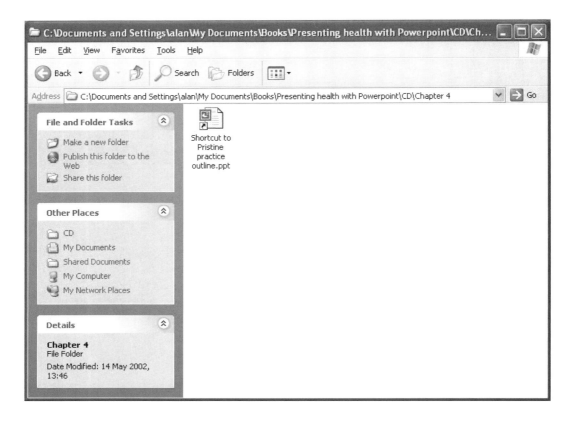

Your first option is to use a pre-defined presentation design. There are many included in PowerPoint.

🖱 Click on Format.

🖱 Click on Slide Design.

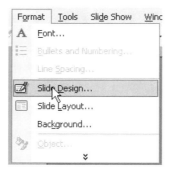

The slide design panel appears at the right-hand side:

🖱 Click on Ocean.pot.

The whole presentation is now re-formatted.

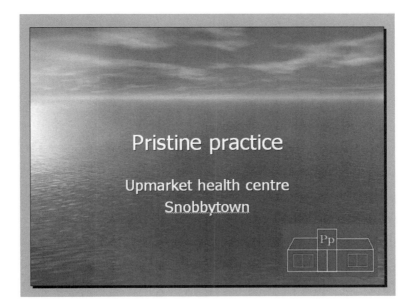

Smart Alec says
'And much better for it: that yellow on turquoise was disgusting. He's colour-blind, you know: did you guess?'

Whilst we're on making things more tasteful, let's get rid of that disgusting logo. The NHS itself has been 're-branding' and we will consider this at the end of this chapter. For now we'll replace the logo with the NHS logo.

Select the Pristine Practice logo.
Press [Del].

Now let's add the NHS logo to the slide master.

CD link
The NHS logo is on the CD, in the Chapter 4 folder, stored as NHSlogo.jpg. The task is a repeat of adding the original logo described in Chapter 3, so it's over to you. The one I prepared earlier is shown below.

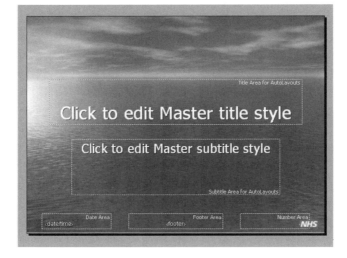

You can use this approach to tailor the design to your own needs, by adding, deleting or changing elements in the design. Just remember to do it in slide master view, so that you make the changes to all the slides.

Alternatively, you can build a design from scratch to meet your own needs, as you did in Chapter 2, only now you can add images, logos and lines and boxes to your heart's content.

NHS house styles

As mentioned above, the NHS has been through a re-branding exercise and has a house style with small variations for local organisations. On the following pages you will find samples of NHS presentation designs.

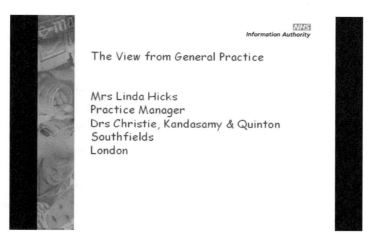

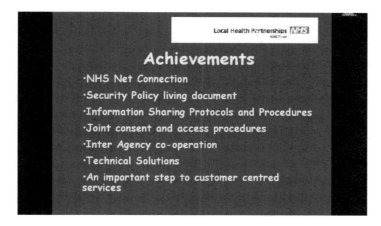

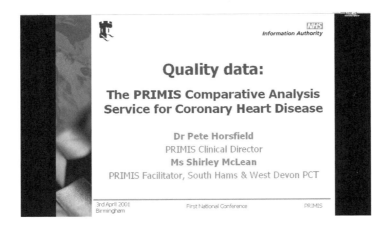

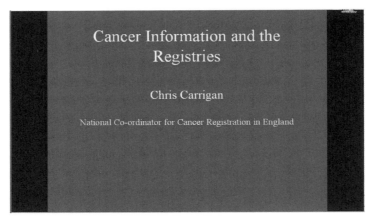

Over to you

Consider the four presentations from the NHS above, and consider the evidence of a house style. See the CD for full colour versions of these.

Complete the table below, and then answer the following questions.

	NHSIA	Partnerships	PRIMIS	Cancer Reg.
Background				
Font type				
Font colour				
Font size				

Questions to think about:

1 How much evidence of a house style is there?
2 How much is desirable?
3 Which presentation is the most attractive?
4 Which presentation fits your preconceptions about the NHS?

CD link
This evaluation form is provided as an Acrobat file on the CD for you to print out and as a Word document if you prefer to fill it in on the screen.

What you should know

By the end of this chapter you should be able to answer the following questions.

• What is a house style?
• Why use a house style?
• What goes into a house style?

You should also know how to set up a house style.

• How to impose a pre-defined presentation design.
• How to modify a pre-defined presentation design.
• How to build a presentation design from scratch.

5

PowerPoint and the World Wide Web

Smart Alec says
'In this chapter he assumes a certain basic knowledge of Internet, mostly that you can use Internet Explorer or Netscape to find a web site on the World Wide Web.
   If you can't, then I'm afraid there are only a few options:

- go and make a cup of coffee, and then go onto Part Two
- do a quick ECDL Internet module.

Have a go anyway: it's not too bad!'

Using the World Wide Web as a source of material

The Internet is a powerful source of material for use in PowerPoint presentations. The first port of call is the official Microsoft web site. The official Microsoft PowerPoint web site is at:

- http://www.microsoft.com/office/powerpoint/default.asp

CD link
From the CD accompanying this book you can link to
this site via the World Wide Web.

To get to this page:

Double-click on Internet Explorer or Netscape on your desktop

Type 'http://www.microsoft.com/office/powerpoint/default.asp' in the
Address bar.

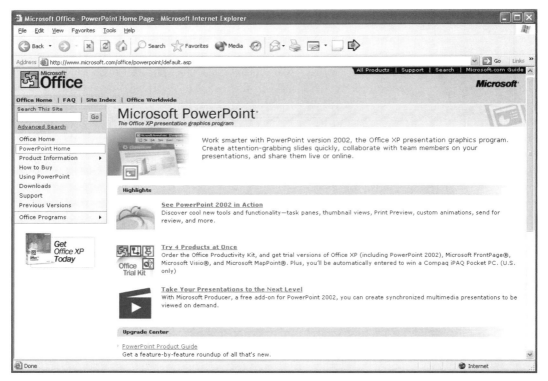

Here you can access a range of resources including:

• add-on resources
• clip art
• templates

and so on . . .

Smart Alec says
'Remember to scroll down, as most of the useful stuff is at the bottom of the page.'

Upgrade Center

PowerPoint Product Guide
Get a feature-by-feature roundup of all that's new.

Office XP Demo: See It to Believe It
Watch this interactive demo, and experience the smarter way to work.

Test-Drive Office XP and PowerPoint 2002
Order the 30-day Office XP trial CD, which includes PowerPoint 2002.

How to Buy
Ready to order? Here's how.

Tools to Help You Work Smarter in PowerPoint 2002

Tips & Tricks: Save time with PowerPoint shortcuts

Templates: Got writer's block? Find the cure at the Template Gallery

Tutorials: Complete tasks faster with help from the Assistance Center

Clip Art: Add pizzazz to your presentation with art from the Design Gallery Live

Books: Find PowerPoint learning materials on eShop

Downloads: Update your software at the Office Download Center

There are other resources from third parties, too.
   To find some of them:

⌨ type 'http://www.google.com' into your browser
⌨ type 'PowerPoint' in the dialog box

   click on Google Search

and a veritable treasure trove awaits you:

Category: Computers > Software > Presentation > Microsoft Powerpoint

PowerPoint Viewer 97 for **PowerPoint** 97, 2000, and 2002 Users
... **PowerPoint** Viewer 97 for **PowerPoint** 97, 2000, and 2002 Users. This
download is for users who don't have Microsoft **PowerPoint®**; it ...
office.microsoft.com/downloads/2000/Ppview97.aspx - 23k - 8 Aug 2002 - Cached - Similar pages

Office Tools on the Web - Page Not Found (404)
Microsoft Office Office Tools on the Web - page not found. Sorry, there
is no office.microsoft.com Web page matching your request. ...
office.microsoft.com/2000/downloaddetails/xlviewer.htm - 4k - 8 Aug 2002 - Cached - Similar pages
[More results from office.microsoft.com]

Microsoft Office - **PowerPoint** Home Page
... Work smarter with **PowerPoint** version 2002, the Office XP presentation
graphics program. Create attention-grabbing slides quickly ...
www.microsoft.com/office/powerpoint/default.asp - 33k - 8 Aug 2002 - Cached - Similar pages

Microsoft Office Converters and Viewers
... your files. To find the viewers and converters you need, simply select
the program for the file you want to share. ... To top of page, ...
www.microsoft.com/office/000/viewers.htm - 21k - 8 Aug 2002 - Cached - Similar pages
[More results from www.microsoft.com]

PowerPoint in the Classroom
... **PowerPoint** in the Classroom is produced by ACT360 Media Ltd. in conjunction with
Microsoft Corporation. Copyright ACT360 Media Ltd., 1998. All rights reserved.
Description: Students of all ages can create multimedia presentations using Microsoft **PowerPoint**. Teach them how...
Category: Computers > Software > Presentation > Microsoft Powerpoint
www.actden.com/pp/ - 4k - Cached - Similar pages

PowerPoint Tutorial
PowerPoint Tutorial. This tutorial is copyrighted by the Department
of Computer Science at The University of Rhode Island. ...
homepage.cs.uri.edu/tutorials/ csc101/powerpoint/ppt.html - 2k - Cached - Similar pages

Microsoft Office
Microsoft Office, The page you are trying to reach has moved. Please
update your bookmarks with the new URL. http://office.microsoft ...
Category: Computers > Software > Operating Systems > Windows > Updates and Service Packs
officeupdate.microsoft.com/ - 3k - Cached - Similar pages

The **PowerPoint** FAQ List
... RECORD A VIDEO of a presentation. Printing from **PowerPoint**. Print without
opening **PowerPoint**. Taking it to the Web. ... PROGRAMMING **POWERPOINT**. ...
Description: Frequently asked questions including techniques, how-to information, troubleshooting, and links to...
Category: Computers > Software > Presentation > Microsoft Powerpoint
www.rdpslides.com/pptfaq/ - 45k - 8 Aug 2002 - Cached - Similar pages

The Gettysburg **Powerpoint** Presentation
The Gettysburg **Powerpoint** Presentation. 11/19/1863. And now please
welcome President Abraham Lincoln. Uh, good morning. Just a second ...
www.norvig.com/Gettysburg/ - 3k - Cached - Similar pages

PowerPoint Tips
At a Bit Better, we happen to know a LOT about **PowerPoint**. ... MIS managers might
enjoy the list of system requirements. **PowerPoint** Presentations. ...
www.bitbetter.com/powertips.htm - 28k - Cached - Similar pages

Goooooooooogle ▶
Result Page: **1** 2 3 4 5 6 7 8 9 10   **Next**

Over to you
There's lots of stuff to explore here. And if you think this is all American-oriented, try doing the same search at:

* http://www.google.co.uk/

Provided you select the UK only option, the results should be more local in nature.

However, we can use the Web directly to find resources for us. Supposing you fancy a brick wall as a background.

Type 'http://www.google.com' in the browser Address bar.
Type brick in the 'google' dialog box.
Click on 'images' to search for images instead of pages.
Click on Google Search.

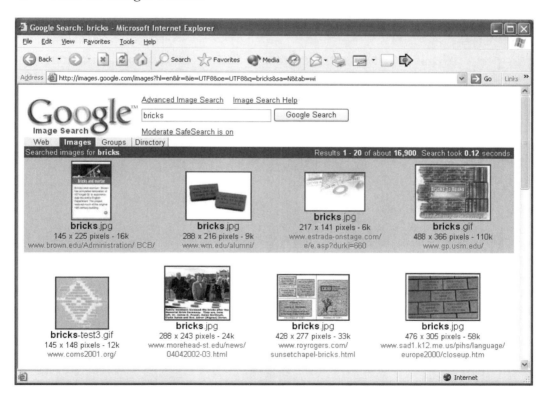

Now we have to be a bit creative.

Click on bricks.gif at the top right-hand corner.

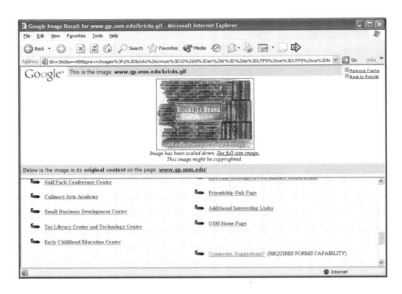

We want to select a section of the brick wall to use as a texture in PowerPoint. To do this:

☞ press [Alt] and [PrtSc] together to save the active window as an image.

Next we have to select the Paint application from the Start menu.

🖱 Click on ⊞ start .
🖱 Select All Programs.

🖑 Select Accessories.
🖑 Select Paint.

This is the Windows Paint application, a simple but useful way to manipulate images.

A blank canvas appears when you first open the application.

🖑 Click on Edit.
🖑 Click on Paste.

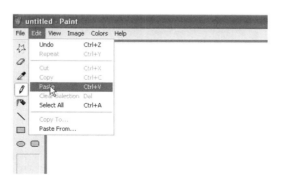

The screenshot appears in the Paint window.

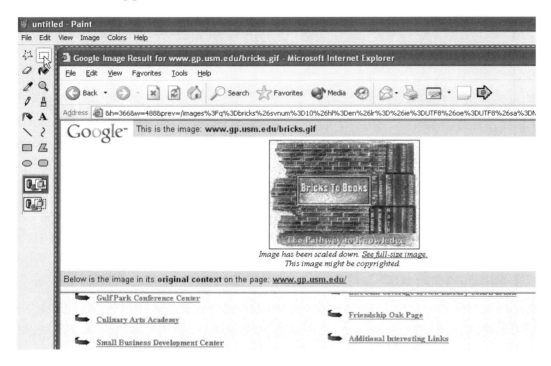

Next we need to extract a small section of the bricks to act as our background texture. To do this it's useful to zoom in on the required section.

🖰 Click on View.
🖰 Click on Zoom.
🖰 Click on Large Size.

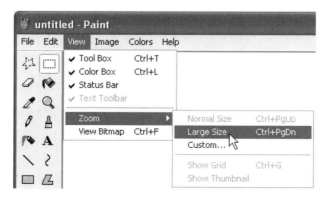

The result may be a little confusing but it allows precise manipulation.

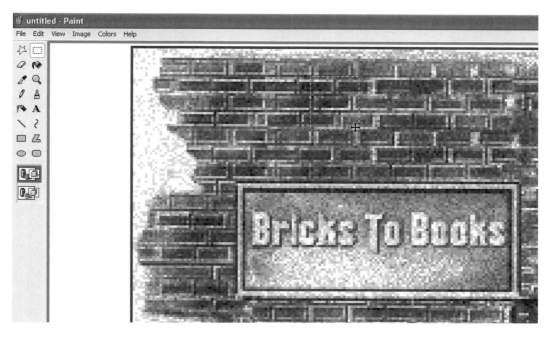

 Click on the selection tool (top right of the toolbox).
 Drag an area to be selected.

Smart Alec says
'In order to get a nice brick wall, you need to select a section which looks like this:'

 Click on Edit.
 Click on Copy.
 Click on File.
 Click on New.
 Click on Edit.
 Click on Paste.

and you should end up with a nice little brick pattern:

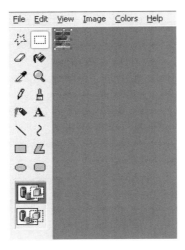

✍ Click on File.
✍ Click on Save As.

Save the file as bricks.jpg in 'My Pictures'.

✍ Click on Save.

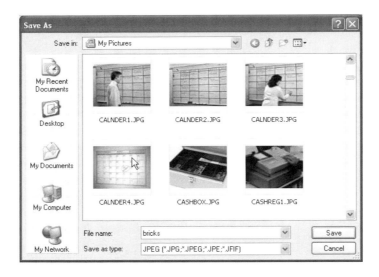

Now we can use it as a background to a PowerPoint presentation.

✍ Open a new PowerPoint presentation.
✍ Click on Format.
✍ Click on Background.

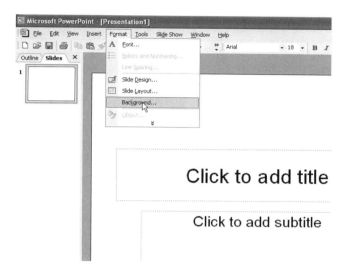

⏳ Click on the drop-down below the Background fill box:

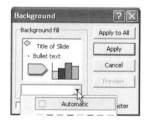

⏳ Click on Fill Effects.
⏳ Click on the Texture tab.

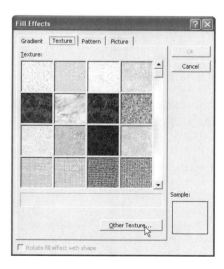

✓🕮 Click on Other Texture.

✓🕮 Select bricks.jpg from the My Pictures folder.

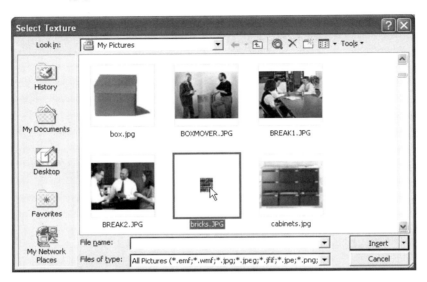

✓🕮 Click on Insert.

The bricks are added to the list of available textures. Make sure it is highlighted and then:

✓🕮 click on OK.

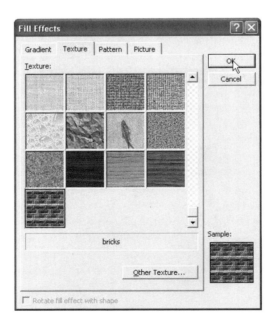

✓🖮 Click on Apply to all to apply this background to the whole presentation.

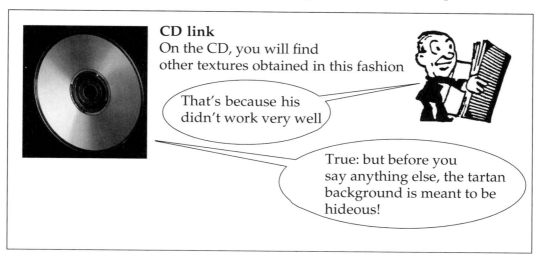

The other thing you can source from the Web is actual images to use in your presentations.

For example, supposing you need a picture of some pills:

⌨ type 'http://www.google.com' in the browser Address bar
⌨ type 'pills' in the Google dialog box
✓🖮 click on images to search for images instead of pages
✓🖮 click on Google search.

Just the first page of the Google search produces a range of images of pills.

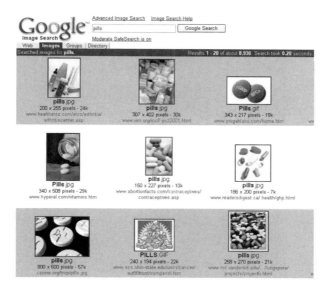

Smart Alec says
'DO NOT BREAK THE LAW!
    Always make sure that any images that you use are either in the public domain or that you have permission to use them if they are copyright images.
    Do not assume that because they are on the Web they are copyright free!'

Subject to legal limitations, you can gather a wide range of images from the Web.

Using the World Wide Web as a publishing medium

In the last section, we looked at getting information from the Web to enhance our presentations. However, the Web is a great place to publish your presentation.

Over to you
To investigate what's out there, go to the NHSIA website at:

• http://www.nhsia.nhs.uk/

and search the site using the search facility for PowerPoint presentations. This will reveal all sorts of presentations and some of them may even be interesting!

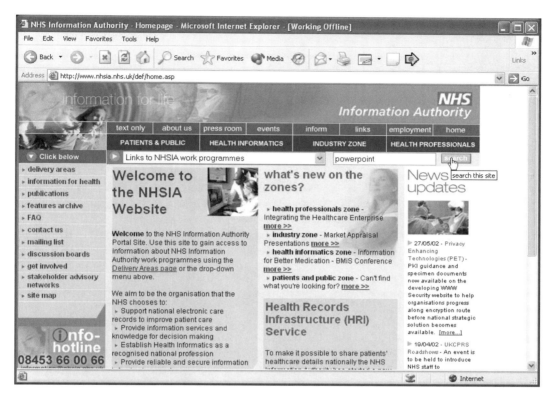

To publish a presentation on the Web, you normally first save it as web pages. We shall use our Pristine Practice presentation as an example.

CD link
If you can't find yours then go to the Chapter 3 folder on the CD and open the presentation.

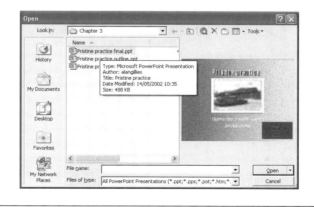

✓🖰 Click on File.

✓🖰 Click on Save As.

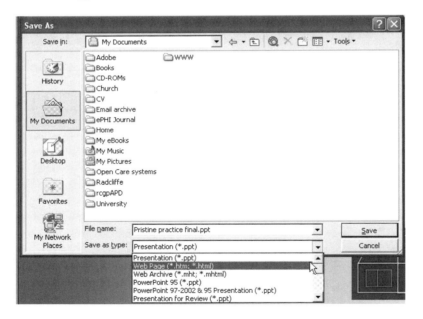

Find a suitable folder in My Documents and then save the presentation in Web Page format.

✍ Click on <u>S</u>ave.

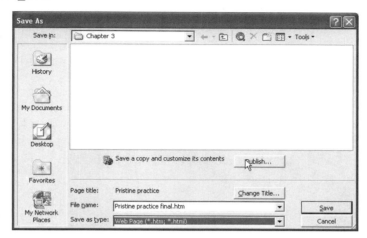

You now have the option of customising your presentation. If you don't want to change anything, you can simply click on <u>S</u>ave. If, however, you think you might want to change something:

✍ click on <u>P</u>ublish.

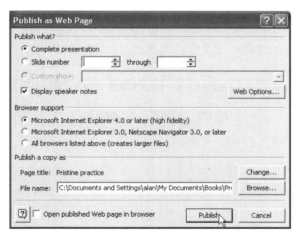

Here you can edit the presentation, change the title that appears and much more.

Over to you
To investigate the options, have a play!
    When you're happy with it:

✍ click on <u>P</u>ublish.

The web pages will now appear in the folder you selected. They are not yet on the Web. However, if you want to put them on the Web, you will need to find some space on a server and load your files onto it. But that's another book . . .

The other thing you can do is load up your PowerPoint presentation as it is and if someone has PowerPoint on their machine they'll be able to access it as a PowerPoint presentation.

CD link
To see how this works, go to the CD in Explorer and double-click on the file marked 'Demo web page' in the Chapter 5 folder.

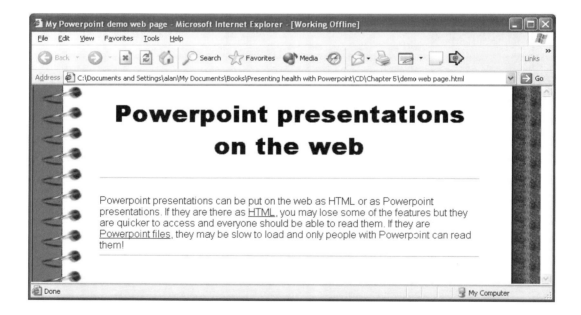

🖰 Click on the <u>HTML</u> hyperlink.

You will see the presentation as HTML pages:

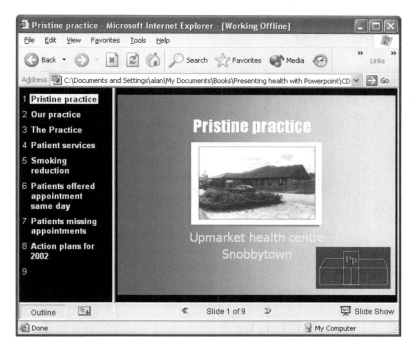

Alternatively:

🖰 click on the <u>PowerPoint files</u> hyperlink.

This shows you the presentation in its original format, once you get past the dialog box:

 Click on <u>O</u>pen to access the presentation:

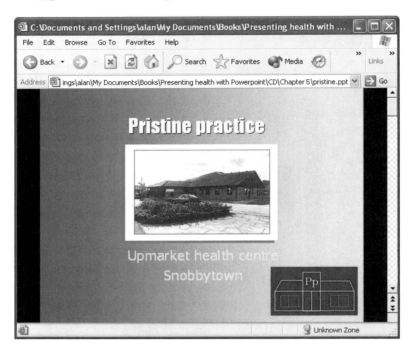

If you page through this presentation you will find that this has retained the original audio and transitional features of the presentation.

 **Smart Alec says**
'For those of you with anorak-wearing credentials and smart people like me, I've pinched the HTML code for his demo page to show you:'

```
<HTML>
<HEAD>
<TITLE>My PowerPoint demo web page</TITLE>
<link rel=stylesheet href =''look1.css'' type=''text/css''>
</HEAD>
<BODY>
<TABLE BORDER=0 WIDTH=690>
<TR><TD WIDTH=90></TD>
<TD WIDTH=600>
<CENTER><H1>PowerPoint presentations on the web</H1></CENTER>
```

```
<HR>
<P>PowerPoint presentations can be put on the web as HTML or
as PowerPoint presentations. If they are there as <A HREF=
''Pristine practice final.htm''> HTML</A>, you may lose some of
the features but they are quicker to access and everyone should
be able to read them. If they are <A HREF=''pristine.ppt''>
PowerPoint files</A>, they may be slow to load and only people
with PowerPoint can read them!<HR></TD>
</TR></TABLE></HTML>
```

What you should know

By the end of this chapter you should know how to use the World Wide Web to enhance presentations by:

- searching for material on the World Wide Web
- importing material from the World Wide Web

and how to use the World Wide Web to publish presentations:

- as HTML
- as a full PowerPoint presentation.

Part Two: Talking and using PowerPoint

6

How not to ruin a presentation with PowerPoint

Introduction

I was sitting in a conference recently. In true academic spirit, the conference was taking place far from home in a beautiful city with wonderful restaurants and a great climate and trams. In spite of all of these positive factors and the undoubted prestige of the conference, it was impossible to ignore the fact that most of the presentations were very poor and many were downright boring!

In this part of the book we shall seek to make your presentations less boring. In this chapter we consider the mechanics of PowerPoint presentations.

Avoiding mistakes: follow the information highway code

The first step to achieving success is to avoid failure. There are some common errors to avoid.

Rule 1: Less is more

Never put more than five points on one slide

If you find yourself in breach of this rule, best practice is to say less and remove some text. Alternatively, make two slides.

Rule 2: Less is more (again)

Keep each point short; use no more than six words per point

If you find yourself in breach of this rule, best practice is to say less and remove some text. Alternatively, make two slides.

Rule 3: Less is more (again)

Don't have too many slides, not more than one slide per 2 minutes talking (120 seconds)

If you find yourself in breach of this rule, best practice is to say less and remove a slide or two.

Here are three versions of a slide, all of which are based on slides I have seen at conferences.

1   A really bad slide:

ON THE COMPUTERIZATION OF GENERAL PRACTICE IN THE UK: THE IT PERSPECTIVE

Alan Gillies, MA PhD. Lancashire Business School, PRESTON. PR1 2HE.

Abstract

This paper is concerned with the computerization of the primary health care sector in the United Kingdom. This care is provided by family doctors, known as General Practitioners (GPs). The sector has been transformed in the years since 1986 by a series of legislative changes. These changes have had profound implications for the information requirements of GPs. They have led to the widespread adoption of computerised patient record systems by GPs rising from less than 25% before 1988, to greater than 75% by 1993.

The paper considers evidence from a variety of historical surveys and combines this with first-hand experience drawn from working to implement information technology (IT) in the NHS and through a set of interviews carried out for this study.

It seeks to evaluate the process up to the present, and to identify critical factors relevant to both practitioners and IT professionals who are increasingly involved with the National Health Service (NHS) in the UK.The paper considers evidence from a variety of historical surveys and combines this with first-hand experience drawn from working to implement information technology (IT) in the NHS and through a set of interviews carried out for this study. It seeks to evaluate the process up to the present, and to identify critical factors relevant Finally, it makes recommendations for both health and IT professionals on the future IT needs of general practice.

2   A rather cluttered slide:

ON THE COMPUTERIZATION OF GENERAL PRACTICE IN THE UK: THE IT PERSPECTIVE

Alan Gillies, MA PhD. Lancashire Business School, PRESTON. PR1 2HE.

Summary

- **Rise in GP computerisation**
- **Evaluates impact of growth in computerisation through**
  - ➢ **Literature review**
  - ➢ **Live case study**
- **Recommendations for future policy**

3   Two focused slides:

ON THE COMPUTERIZATION OF GENERAL PRACTICE IN THE UK: THE IT PERSPECTIVE

Alan Gillies, MA PhD. Lancashire Business School, PRESTON.
PR1 2HE.

Summary

- **Rise in GP computerisation**
- **Evaluates impact of growth in computerisation through:**
  - **Literature review**
  - **Live case study**
- **Recommendations for future policy**

There are some other ways to ruin a good presentation. Look at my next version of the above slide:

Summary

- Rise in GP computerisation
- Evaluates impact of growth in computerisation through:
  - Literature review
  - Live case study
- *Recommendations for future policy*

Which brings us to Rule 4!

Rule 4: Less is more (again)

Don't use more than two fonts, and don't mix serif and sans serif fonts

Times New Roman is an example of a serif font
Arial is an example of a sans serif font

Rule 5: Less is more (again)

Do not use all the same case, as it's easier to read a mixture of upper and lower case

Look at the slides below and decide which is the easiest to read.

1   The upper case for investment

> ### CAPITAL INVESTMENT PLANS
> - THE TRUST PLANS TO INVEST £10.6 MILLION IN CAPITAL PROJECTS DURING 2002-03
> - THE TRUST IS SEEKING TO OBTAIN 50% OF THIS THROUGH PFI INITIATIVES
> - SOME BOARD MEMBERS HAVE QUESTIONED THE CASE FOR PFI
> - THE INCREASED USE OF PFI REMAINS A GOVERNMENT IMPERATIVE

2   The lower case for investment

> ### capital investment plans
> - the trust plans to invest £10.6 million in capital projects during 2002-03
> - the trust is seeking to obtain 50% of this through pfi initiatives
> - some board members have questioned the case for pfi
> - the increased use of pfi remains a government imperative

3   The mixed case for investment

Capital Investment Plans

- The Trust plans to invest £10.6 million in capital projects during 2002-03

- The Trust is seeking to obtain 50% of this through PFI initiatives

- Some board members have questioned the case for PFI

- The increased use of PFI remains a Government imperative

Rule 6: Less is more (again)
Keep diagrams simple

So, if I can't read it, why are you including it?

Complex diagrams are illegible. They often include text which is too small in upper and lower case, and are offered with the feeble excuse: I know you can't read this at the back

And so to colour. This is difficult because:

1   I'm colour-blind!
2   This book is black and white.

Rule 7: Less is more (again)

Avoid bright colours

Subtlety is a virtue (not always encouraged by PowerPoint!). Avoid bright colours, especially in large amounts, as they can be distracting, tiring and irritating to viewers.

There are a number of good principles to follow.

- Ensure good contrast between text and background.
- Try near-black (e.g. navy blue) for text and pastel colours for backgrounds (e.g. pale yellow), although an available alternative is pale text on dark blue colours.
- If you have colour vision problems (I do!) check your proposed schemes with a

colleague, preferably female as they are much less likely to have such problems.

- Avoid complementary colours in combination, such as red and green or blue and orange.
- Projection devices such as data projectors and LCDs often display colours in quite a different way than a monitor. Always try to check your presentation in the display environment to avoid unpleasant surprises!

Smart Alec says
'Most of the supplied templates in PowerPoint are OK these days, but there were some truly awful designs in the past in early versions.'

And finally to patterns and backgrounds.

Rule 8: Less is more (again)

Complex patterns can seem like a good idea but can be extremely harmful!

At best they can be distracting and at worst they can completely obliterate the message. If you don't like a flat background, why not use a graded background as provided in PowerPoint?

Compare the following sides of the same slide. I have used a standard texture from the PowerPoint application. You can make far more extreme examples by using really busy graphics.

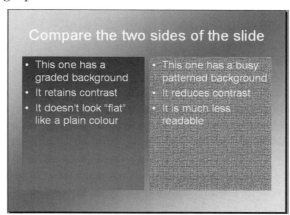

CD link
To see the actual slide in all its glory go to the Chapter 6 folder of the CD and open 'busybackground.ppt'.

Rule 9: Less is more (again)

Don't have too many whizzy transitions

Animation is great fun but too much can weary very quickly. Have a look at 'reallysilly.ppt' in the Chapter 6 folder of the CD.

Smart Alec says
'Don't forget what you learnt in earlier chapters about house styles and consistency. Use a PowerPoint design template to provide a consistent framework.'

Some good things to do

If you follow the information highway code you should avoid the equivalent of a bad smash on the road. However, you can still come up with a very bland and boring presentation. The actual highway code is not a set of laws, it is advisory. So is ours. A more appropriate analogy might be a clinical guideline. They represent good practice. They also represent the lowest common denominator and will not facilitate the best care for all patients. A clinician who follows guidelines without taking any account of the individual patient will fail to deliver the best care.

Therefore we are going to consider when it is a good thing to break the rules to liven up the presentation. Before we do so, there is one final rule or guideline.

Rule 10: Less is more (again)

It is good to break the rules a bit, but it should be done sparingly!

A completely uniform PowerPoint presentation is extremely boring, but variation is used most effectively in small doses.

FIXED PENALTY NOTICE

It's worthwhile breaking up the uniformity of layout. A simple example would be to use a relevant quotation or definition to follow a summary page which is bulleted:

Contents

- What I'm going to say
- What I'm saying
- What I said
- The implications of what I said
- Any questions

The art of boring an audience silly

"If you really want to bore an audience silly, then tell them what you're going to say, then actually tell them, then summarise it, then discuss the implications, making sure at each stage that what you're saying is on the screen in Powerpoint as well"

Smart Alec, 2002

Retaining uniformity of text colour, size and typeface but changing the shape provides reassurance without sending your audience to sleep!

An alternative break in the routine is provided by a diagram or graphic, but remember: keep it simple!

Consider, for example, the following examples from earlier in the book. Remember the organisational charts from Chapter 3? All of the examples shown in that chapter result in text that is too small to read. Better to use a simpler chart and put the detail in the notes accompanying the slide, whether used as a prompt for the speaker or given as a handout:

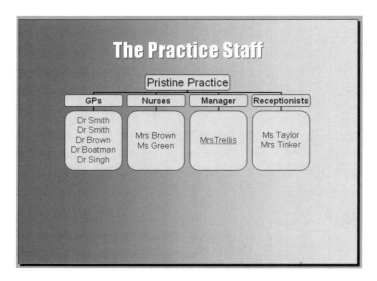

From the same presentation, compare the simple and fussy versions of a bar chart:

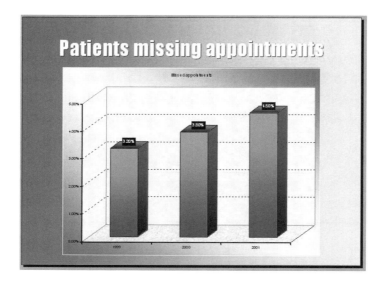

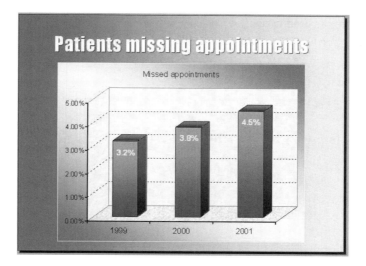

The latest version of PowerPoint has many more subtle effects and backgrounds. However, just occasionally it's worth using a fancy effect. I wanted to convey the idea of a dot representing a point within a 3-D shape on what was obviously a flat slide. The slide is shown below:

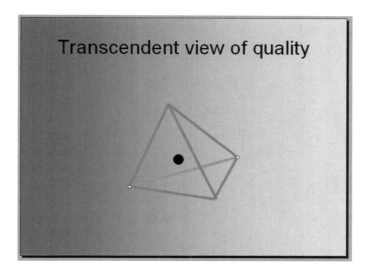

I used a spiral entrance transition effect to enhance the 3-D effect. Look at '3deffect.ppt' in the Chapter 6 section of the CD to see whether you think it worked.

Once you have opened the file:

press [F5] to see the show

click the mouse to watch the dot fly in.

A few (remember: less is more!) party tricks never go amiss. Have a look at party time in Chapter 9 for some more ideas about how to break up the monotony!

What you should know

By the time you have read this chapter, you should know nine things *not* to do in presentations:

- put too many lines of text on a slide
- put too many words on a line
- put too many slides in a presentation
- mix sans serif and serif fonts
- use all the same case
- use complex diagrams
- use lots of bright colours
- use complicated graphical backgrounds
- use lots of 'exciting' transitions.

You should also have engraved on your brain that less is more, but that sometimes it's OK, even necessary, to break the guidelines a bit, otherwise things get very boring!

7

Talking with PowerPoint

Why use PowerPoint at all?

In view of some of the comments thus far, you might assume that I think PowerPoint is a bad idea. On the contrary, I think it's one of the most productive and enjoyable applications in common use. It does, however, illustrate the old maxim:

'To err is human, but it takes a computer to really screw things up.'

PowerPoint is a tool which may be used for good or ill. In this chapter, we shall consider why PowerPoint sometimes makes presentations worse and how we can try to ensure that actually it makes them better.

Why I think many talks with PowerPoint are so boring

When you first learn to speak in public, you will often start by writing speeches in full. As you become more confident, you may depend upon notes as guides rather than a full verbatim text. Finally, you may dispense with the hints altogether.

Very often, people use their PowerPoint presentation as a kind of poor man's autocue. They anxiously click the mouse to see what comes up next to remind them of where they are. They can become as tied to their PowerPoint as a novice speaker is to the script in front of them. Two things can make this even worse:

- if they do not have a handout of the presentation, they may not remember what the next slide says
- if the presentation has lots of whizzy effects, then they may not be sure what is going to happen, even on the current slide: do they need to click, or will it come up automatically? Do the text bullets come up en masse or one at a time?

Speakers seem to think that the PowerPoint presentation is the talk, instead of thinking about what they want to say and how PowerPoint may enhance their talk. PowerPoint may enhance a talk in a number of ways:

- it can act as an aide-memoire
- it can provide visual illustration of an image, data or an idea
- it can entertain the audience
- it can provide a permanent record or summary for the audience.

All of these roles are in fact subservient to the talk itself, and can detract from the primary task of communicating verbally a message. Several years ago, I stopped taking a bulky single lens reflex camera on trips and holidays, as capturing the photographic record had started to overshadow the experiences that it was supposed to capture. The same thing appears to happen with PowerPoint on occasions.

In the last chapter, Alec suggested that the traditional maxim of:

- tell them what you're going to say
- say it
- tell them what you've said

which represents a triplication of the message, has in fact become a hexiplication.

Smart Alec says
'Is hexiplication really a word?'

What he means is that by the time you've said it three times and shown it three times in PowerPoint that's a total of *six* times, and few messages will stand that much repetition!

If you are reinforcing the verbal message with a written version on the slides, you do not need to reinforce it in the verbal presentation to the same extent.

Finally, most books will tell you the principles of good presentation design, but not point out that actually if you don't ever bend them, the presentation will become very bland and boring!

In the rest of the chapter, we shall describe an approach to using PowerPoint which works for me. It may be helpful to you. If not, I apologise.

Planning a presentation with PowerPoint

When I started out on a teacher training course many years ago, they told me that 90% of a good lesson was in the preparation. Since then I have decided that if anything this is an underestimate. PowerPoint can help you plan your talk and especially to structure your thoughts.

CD link
I have written a PowerPoint presentation to help you plan your presentations. It is accessible in the Chapter 7 section of the CD as 'Presentation Planning tool.ppt'.

The presentation provides an outline for the process of designing your talk. To complete each slide requires you to answer a key question about it.

Presentation planning tool

What is the aim of my talk?

The aim of my talk is to:

Who are my target audience?

The main target audience for my talk is:

The secondary target audience for my talk is:

What do they know?

I assume they will have an expert knowledge of:

I assume they will have a basic knowledge of:

The key messages of my talk are

1
2
3
4
5

I will use PowerPoint to

act as an aide memoire ❏
provide visual illustration of an image, data, or an idea ❏
entertain the audience ❏
provide a permanent record or summary for the audience ❏

(tick as appropriate)

I will provide evidence for my talk through

empirical data ❏
supporting literature ❏
personal experience ❏
cartoons ❏
other ❏

(tick as appropriate)

The take home message

The key thought I want to leave in the minds of the audience is:

For a recent talk on paperless practice in primary care, the completed design looked like this:

Presentation Planning Tool

What is the aim of my talk?

The aim of my talk is to explain the pros and cons of paperless practice to GPs.

Who is my target audience?

The main target audience for my talk are GPs

The secondary target audience for my talk is practice managers, practice staff and PCT staff.

What do they know?

I assume they will have an expert knowledge of . . .
I assume they will have a basic knowledge of . . .

The key messages of my talk are

1   Paperless practice is coming whether we like it or not
2   It can be made to work for staff and patients
3   IT is not a magic bullet solution
4   Patients' interests must be paramount
5   Education and training is vital

I will use PowerPoint to

act as an aide-memoire   ☑
provide visual illustration of an image, data, or an idea   ☑
entertain the audience   ☑
provide a permanent record or summary for the audience   ☑

(tick as appropriate)

I will provide evidence for my talk through

empirical data   ☑
supporting literature   ☑
personal experience   ☑

---

cartoons ❏

other ❏

(tick as appropriate)

The take home message

The key thought I want to leave in the minds of the audience is:

You must take control of this process to gain the benefits for your patients and your practice.

CD link

There is a completed PowerPoint presentation showing how this plan looks. It is accessible in the Chapter 7 section of the CD as 'Completed Presentation Planning tool.ppt'.

Because PowerPoint makes it easy to develop presentations as you go along it does not always encourage you to plan properly. Smart Alec has a cautionary tale about this.

Smart Alec says

'Once upon a time, there was a clever man. He noticed that computer programs didn't do what people wanted. So he said wouldn't it be good if we could show people what it would look like before we built it? And so he invented prototyping. Prototypes were simple applications that didn't work properly, but looked as if they did, and he found out a lot about how to build the real computer program from them.

However, there was another man who thought he was even cleverer. He had been trained as an accountant. He said 'Why waste all this money on building a whole new program when we can just modify the prototype and stick in the extra bits we need.'

He tried it and it worked. He was pleased because it saved money and he made more money. His customers were pleased because they got their product more quickly.

Until after a few weeks, it started to go wrong. So the accountant called in a management consultant who made him very sad by telling him that his program was flawed and would have to be re-written at great expense, and presented him with a big bill of his own to boot!

People said that prototyping was a bad idea and the first clever man was sad because it didn't work because they hadn't followed his instructions.

The moral of this story is that whilst it is OK to use PowerPoint to organise your thoughts, you should always start again before designing your final presentation, otherwise your presentation will reflect the process of collecting your thoughts, rather than the final result of the process.'

Giving a presentation with PowerPoint

The process of developing your actual PowerPoint presentation can be accomplished in a number of ways. Rather than provide a detailed recipe, here are some key points to remember.

- Write your talk first. The talk drives the PowerPoint, not the other way around!
- Choose a design that is understated. Less is more!
- The first slide should set the scene and include the title of your talk, your name, your affiliation and contact details.
- As a general rule there shouldn't be more than 10 slides for a 20 minute talk, 30 for an hour.
- Each key point should be represented in your talk.
- Beware acronyms: they are OK, provided you are confident that your audience has a shared knowledge. Make a note to explain verbally any acronyms that are in doubt.
- Once you have got a first draft, find a friend and ask for comments.

Once you have finalised your presentation, check it for:

- ☑ spelling
- ☑ the guidelines in Chapter 6
- ☑ compatibility with your script.

Smart Alec says
'Remember to check that the proofing language is set correctly. Many Office installations are set by default to English (U.S.). This will lead to errors in spelling for audiences in other countries.

To check or change the language:

✍ click on <u>T</u>ools
✍ click on <u>L</u>anguage.'

You may find the following checklist helpful. You can also use it to check other presentations that you see.

CD link
The checklist is provided in Word and Acrobat formats on the CD in the Chapter 7 folder as 'checklist.doc' and 'checklist.pdf' respectively.

PowerPoint checklist

PowerPoint problem checks

Use this checklist once you have designed your presentation.

1	Have any slides got six or more lines of text on a slide?	Yes ❏	No ❏
2	Have any lines of text got more than six words on a line?	Yes ❏	No ❏
3	Are there more than N/2 slides, where N is the length of the talk in minutes?	Yes ❏	No ❏
4	Does the presentation mix sans serif and serif fonts?	Yes ❏	No ❏
5	Do any slides use all the same case instead of mixed upper and lower case?	Yes ❏	No ❏

6	Do any slides use complex diagrams with illegible text?	Yes ❏	No ❏		
7	Do any slides use complicated graphical backgrounds that render the text illegible?	Yes ❏	No ❏		
8	Does the presentation use lots of bright colours?	Yes ❏	No ❏		
9	Does the presentation use lots of 'exciting' transitions?	Yes ❏	No ❏		
10	Does the presentation show any spelling errors, or has it been spell-checked in an appropriate language?	Yes ❏	No ❏		

A 'yes' answer may not always be a bad thing: but there needs to be a rationale for it, and it needs to be a rarity.

Talk checklist

Use this checklist to assess other people's overall talks with PowerPoint, and to ask a friend to review yours.

1	Was the talk interesting?	Very ❏	Quite ❏	No ❏	Dull ❏	Boring ❏
2	Was the PowerPoint interesting?	Very ❏	Quite ❏	No ❏	Dull ❏	Boring ❏
3	Did the PowerPoint help the talk?	A lot ❏	A bit ❏	No ❏	Hindered ❏	Ruined ❏
4	Did the PowerPoint act as an aide-memoire?	A lot ❏	A bit ❏	No ❏	Hindered ❏	Ruined ❏
5	Did it provide helpful visual illustrations of images, data or ideas?	Many ❏	Some ❏	No ❏	Unhelpful ❏	Useless ❏
6	Did it help to entertain the audience?	A lot ❏	A bit ❏	No ❏	Hindered ❏	Ruined ❏
7	Did it help to provide a permanent record or summary for the audience?	A lot ❏	A bit ❏	No ❏	Hindered ❏	Ruined ❏
8	Was the presenter comfortable with using the technology?	Very ❏	Quite ❏	No ❏	Nervous ❏	Terrified ❏
9	Did the speaker look at the audience?	A lot ❏	A bit ❏	No ❏	Rarely ❏	Never ❏
10a	Are there any features of the presentation you would use?	A lot ❏	Some ❏	No ❏		
10b	Are there any features of the presentation you would avoid?			No ❏	Some ❏	A lot ❏

In this checklist, the more choices you select near the left, the better the presentation

Finally, remember that public speaking and its support with PowerPoint presentations is an art as much as a science. You will learn how to do it better. The more you learn, the more you will know how to depart from the guidelines to good effect.

A notebook is a really good tool. Whenever you present or when you sit and listen to other presentations, make notes on what works and what doesn't, and use it to improve your own future presentations.

Smart Alec says
'At your next appraisal, you'll be able to tell your line manager that you're keeping a reflective learning diary on presentation techniques. But remember it's just a notebook really!'

To start this process, we are going to look at a number of presentations in the next chapter to see how effective they are.

What you should know

By the end of this chapter you should know:

- why you want to use PowerPoint
- why your talk is more than a PowerPoint presentation
- how to plan your talk
- how to use a checklist to evaluate a talk.

8

The PowerPoint gallery: examples of presentations

Sample presentation 1

CD link

To view this presentation in all its glory, look on the CD in the Chapter 8 folder, where you will find it stored as 'sample1.ppt'.

This first presentation is designed to show you what not to do. It's a construct, the sort of thing that a local PCT might produce when looking at how to respond to a local health priority – in this case Coronary Heart Disease – in response to the National Service Framework.

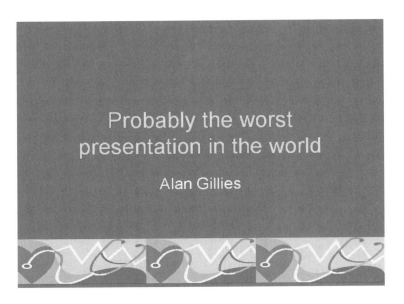

Where to begin? There are major problems here:

- the colour scheme is a combination of bright colours that are designed to have viewers reaching for the paracetamol in under 10 seconds!
- the title tells us nothing about the content of the talk
- the decorative border adds more clashing colours and looks as if it was grabbed from the clip art section using a simplistic keyword search like 'heart'
- the contact details appear and then disappear before anyone has a chance to see them.

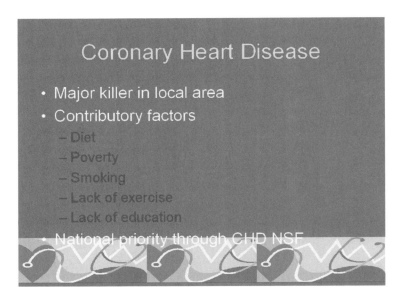

On this slide:

- no introduction
- distracting entrance for the title
- another colour has been introduced, which clashes again
- the final bullet overlaps the border and so is largely unreadable
- NSF as an abbreviation should be OK in health service circles, but should be expanded verbally.

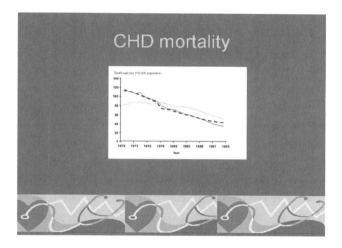

A graph!

- The graph is difficult to read and the trend lines not easy to see.
- Although the lines are differentiated, there is no key.
- Is 1993 the most recent data? Most national data is available in the public domain up to at least five years ago.

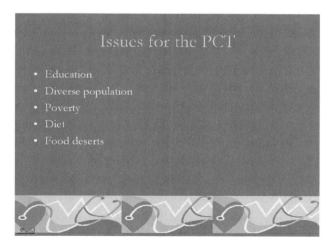

It's another list!

- For some reason, the font has changed, and it's now a serif font. It's also even more difficult to read.
- The points listed are a combination of duplication of the last slide but one, and some new factors with no great rationale for it.

OK, at this point Alec has stepped in and stopped the presentation: it's too awful for words, but I suspect that you may have seen some or all of these problems before.

Sample presentation 2

This is a real presentation, given to the Primary Care Specialist Group of the British Computer Society in Manchester in May 2002. The talk was scheduled for 40 minutes, hence there are 20 slides.

CD link
To view this presentation in all its glory, look on the CD in the Chapter 8 folder where you will find it stored as 'sample2.ppt'

The title slide sets the style for the presentation.

- The aim is to create a sophisticated look with depth which has a subconscious message of 'looking through the window' to find out what's inside. The use of semi-transparent effects and the white brick texture allows complexity without distracting from the text. The text is set on a semi-transparent light blue background as a further aid to clarity.
- The choice of white and blue gives an uncluttered look with high contrast.
- The choice of 'Comic Sans MS' as font is intended to set an informal tone echoed in the talk itself.
- The email address appears on each slide to allow its noting at any point. It is distinguished by use of a different font.

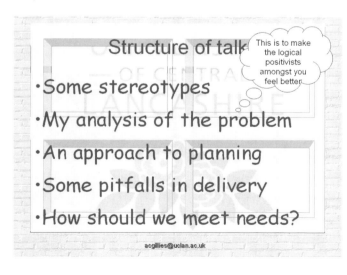

This is a contents page.

- People do like to know where they are going. This is the purpose of this slide.
- The thought bubble tells you that this is why the slide is here, and also adds a little interest to an otherwise dull slide.

This is the first key point of my talk, that training plans are often ad hoc at present. I said this in the presentation so, rather than repeat it on a slide, I reinforced it with a cartoon. A cartoon is used because it's a caricature, which provides a good metaphor for a stereotype.

The same technique is used in the next slide to make the point that decisions may be driven by external pressures:

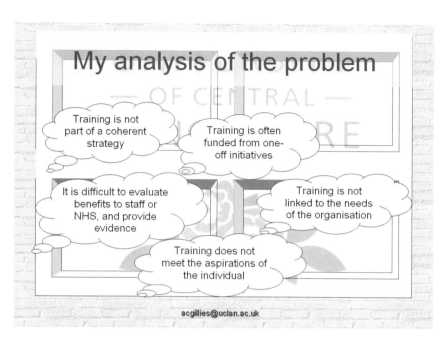

When is a bulleted list not a bulleted list? The use of thought balloons serves two purposes: it provides an alternative to the bog standard bulleted list and reinforces the idea that these are my thoughts on the problem. The next two slides return to a more traditional format . . .

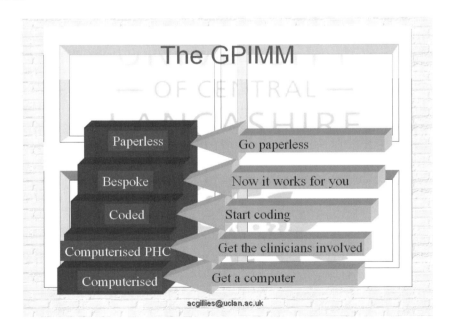

. . . before using a visual animation to display one of the most important concepts in the presentation, the GPIMM model. The importance is emphasised by preceding it with a couple of conventional lists. It also allows the use of a visual staircase metaphor, illustrating the stepwise improvement at the heart of the model.

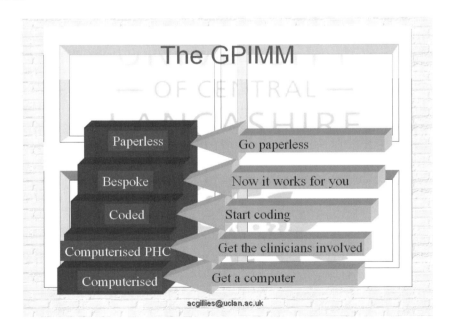

This is followed by a conventional bulleted list:

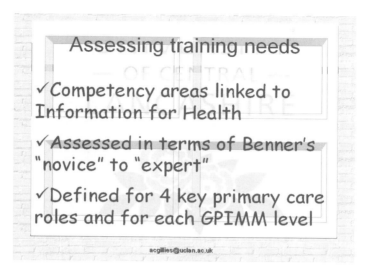

This slide sets out the structure for the next section of the presentation. A small touch is the use of ticks as bullets, emphasising the positive features of the approach.

The next two slides operate as a pair. They illustrate the concept of competence by showing the cases of 'overskilled' and 'underskilled'.

The complementary nature of the concepts is illustrated by the fact that the layout switches, with the graphic on the left of the text at first, and then on the right. This is intended to show how they are two sides of the same coin, a point that is further emphasised by the constant header:

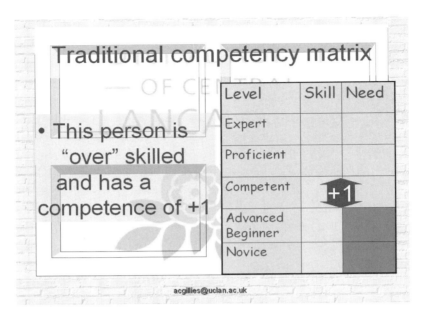

The next slide shows how the approach described builds upon the traditional approach. It uses a dynamic graph to show that as an organisation matures, so its training needs change over time. Although it is a complex slide, the key information is kept in a large font size and the removal of information as the slide develops prevents it from being cluttered. Inevitably, there is some compromise and the labelling of the graph is too small. This was explained in the talk.

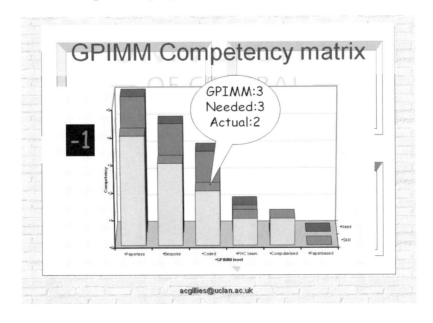

The next slide is a simple bulleted list describing the characteristics of the software tools. This is reinforced by a screenshot of the tools themselves:

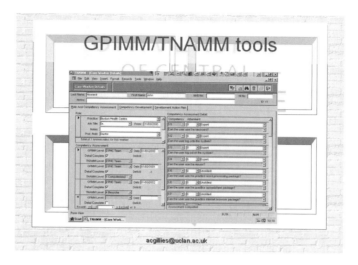

The screenshot is then covered by a text box, advertising a workshop that afternoon:

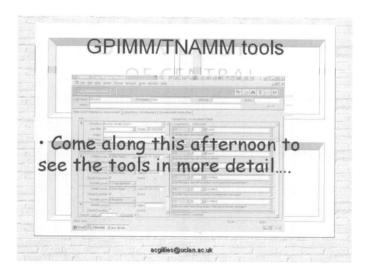

This slide faces the classic problem of putting detail onto the screen. There is no way that a viewer can detect the detail from the slide. The text, however, acknowledges this and tells the viewer how to get the detailed information they seek.

The next couple of slides use traditional bulleted lists to compare the pros and cons of the approach:

Some advantages of this approach

- Facilitates planning
- Ensures training is appropriate and relevant
- Provides evidence of effectiveness of training
- Links training to organisational goals
- Provides evidence for clinical governance

acgillies@uclan.ac.uk

Some pitfalls in application

- Can encourage short term approach
- May emphasise training over education
- May not address staff aspirations
- Needs to be treated as an aid to decision making, rather than gospel truth

acgillies@uclan.ac.uk

As the presentation draws to a close, the next slides are designed to introduce a degree of symmetry, echoing the early cartoon stereotypes:

NB: Note the use of a specific font to suggest a technical, structured approach.

To emphasise the key message that education is preferable to training, the next slide uses a quotation. This results in a text slide with a different shape (*see* Chapter 6).

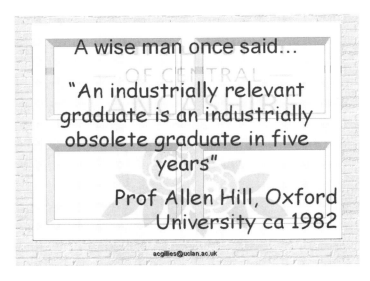

The final slide provides more on the same topic.

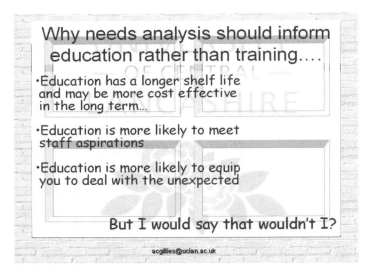

This slide is the final slide and is not a summary of what has been said. This is because:

- I've already said what I'm going to say and said it, and put both of these into the presentation. That's a quadruple reinforcement: that's enough!
- The final message is what they will remember above all: it's an opportunity to send them home with a clear message.
- The use of this technique with a firm take-home message rather than a balanced conclusion is acknowledged in the paraphrase from the Profumo trial.

So to conclude I use a simple 'Thank you'. After all, good manners are usually appreciated!

Over to you
On the CD you will find three of my earlier presentations. Whilst you cannot hear them in the context of the talk, use the checklist from Chapter 7 to evaluate them as far as possible.
   They are in the Chapter 8 folder as:

1   evaluate1.ppt
2   evaluate2.ppt
3   evaluate3.ppt

Smart Alec says
'Don't think that just because he wrote them, they're all perfect or even good; there are some real howlers. Still, perhaps he's learnt something from writing the book!'

What you should know

By the end of this chapter you should have put a lot of the rest of the book, especially Part Two, into practice.

9

Party time!

The use of party tricks

As always, party tricks should be limited in their use, but a few never hurt. Party tricks do not have to be flashy, as the first one will show.

The black screen

This is the simplest trick of all. At the start and end of the presentation it can be really helpful to have a black screen. You can leave it displayed before you talk and after you finish during questions. It prevents the PowerPoint screen becoming a distraction.

To add a black screen to an existing presentation, do as follows:

- press [Ctrl] and [Home] to go to the first slide
- click on Insert
- click on New Slide
- right-click on the slide in the left-hand margin.

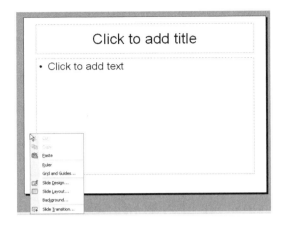

From the short menu:

🖐 click on Back<u>g</u>round
🖐 click on the drop-down box for Background fill colour.

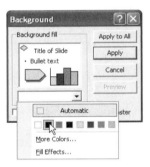

🖐 Select black as the background colour.
🖐 Click on Apply and the slide turns black!

To finish off you need to move this slide, as PowerPoint inserted it after the initial title slide. Look at the left-hand side of the screen. If the text outline is showing:

click on the Slides tab

and then drag the second slide (the black one!) to the top.

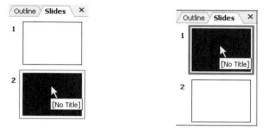

The curtain call

If you think the above a little dull, then try bringing down the curtain on your presentation with the following slide.

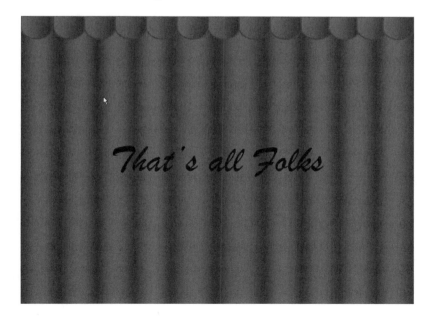

CD link
On the CD you will find the finished slide as 'curtains.ppt' in the Chapter 9 folder.

Start with a blank slide.

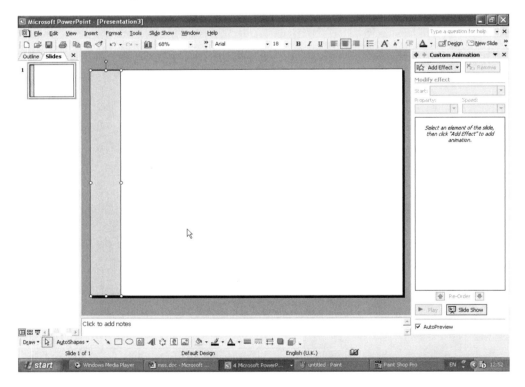

Draw a rectangle at the left-hand side of the slide:

Right-click on the rectangle.

Select Format Autoshape from the short menu.

Set Fill Color to dark red.

From the same menu, select Fill Effects and select Vertical shading, choosing the fourth option as shown (this gives the curtains their nice pleated effect!).

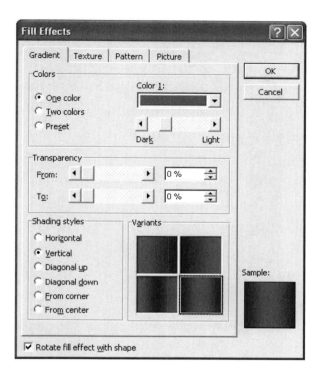

↗🖐 Click on OK.
↗🖐 Select No Line as the line colour.

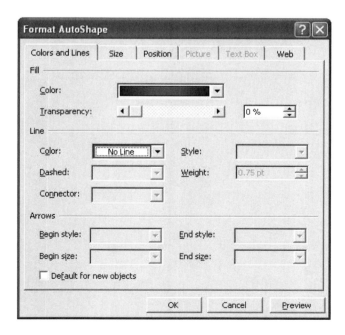

🖑 Click on OK.

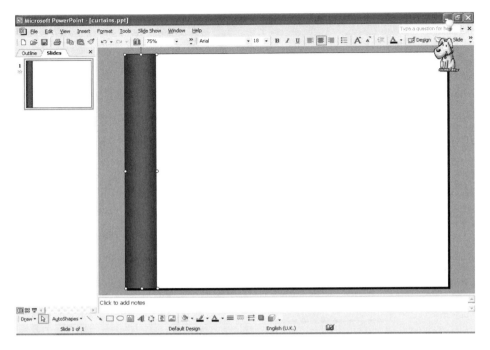

Now we copy this rectangle to the right-hand side of the slide.

🖑 Click on 📄 .
🖑 Click on 📋 .
🖑 Drag the pasted shape across to the right-hand side:

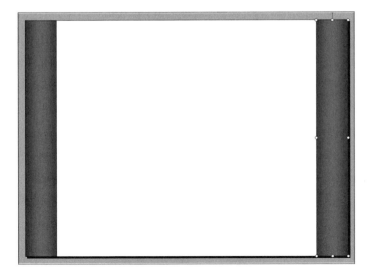

Repeat this process, building up the curtains by pasting copies of the original shape in the following order:

	2	4	6	8	9	7	5	3	1

When you insert the last two panes, you may need to stretch them so that they meet in the centre:

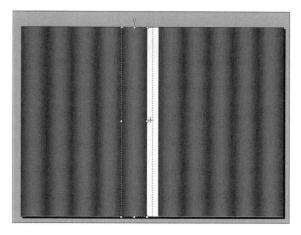

The finished result should show no gaps:

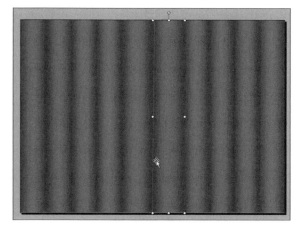

Next we need to add the transitions to draw the curtains.

✓🖰 Select the curtains on the left-hand side of the slide:

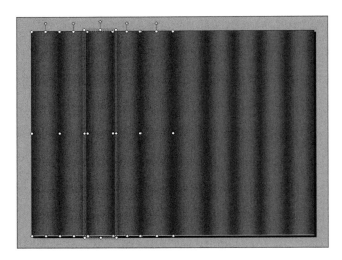

✓🖰 Click on Slide Show.
✓🖰 Click on Custom Animation.

The Custom Animation dialog appears on the right-hand side of the screen.

✓🖰 Click on Add Effect.

🖱 Click on Entrance.
🖱 Click on 9. Stretch.

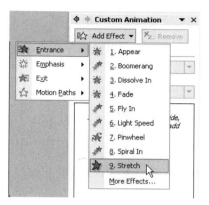

🖱 Select On Click as the Start option.
🖱 Select From Left as the Direction.
🖱 Select Medium as the speed.

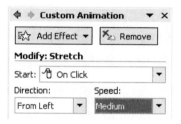

Repeat the process for the right-hand side panels. The only exception is that the Direction should be From Right.

This completes the basic curtains. The version on the CD has two refinements, a message and a decorative frill at the top of the curtains. To add the text, we need to add a text box.

🖱 Click on ▣ on the drawing toolbar.
🖱 Type 'That's all Folks'.

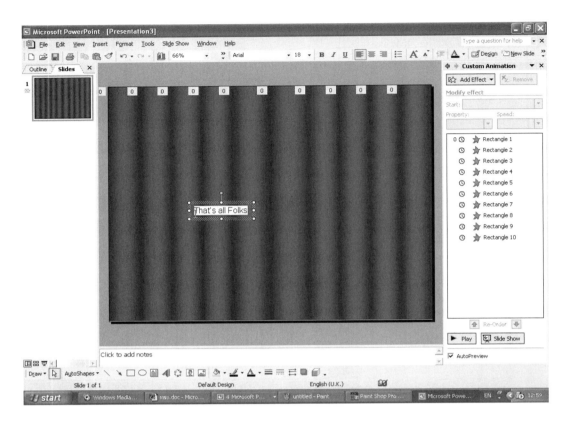

Next we need to align and format the text.

The text used in the example is 72pt Brush Script. You can make this modification using the format toolbar at the top of the screen:

To align it correctly:

- click on Draw
- click on Align or Distribute
- click on Relative to Slide
- click on Draw
- click on Align or Distribute
- click on Align Center
- click on Draw

🖐 click on Align or Distribute
🖐 click on Align Middle.

And finally, add the decoration at the top.

🖐 Click on Autoshapes.
🖐 Click on Flowchart.
🖐 Click on the symbol for delay.

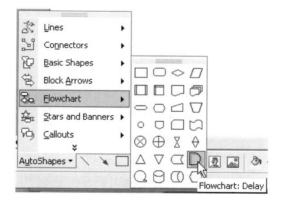

🖐 Drag the symbol to the size you need.
🖐 Click on Draw.
🖐 Click on Rotate or Flip.
🖐 Click on Rotate Right.
🖐 Drag it up to the top left-hand corner of the slide.
🖐 Right click on the symbol.
🖐 Select Format Autoshape from the short menu.
🖐 Set Fill Color to dark red.
🖐 Select Fill Effects and select Horizontal shading, choosing the second option as shown:

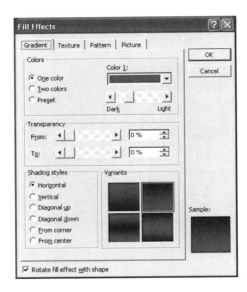

〽 Click on OK to return to the previous dialog.

〽 Select a darker red shade as the line colour and 2.5pt as the line thickness:

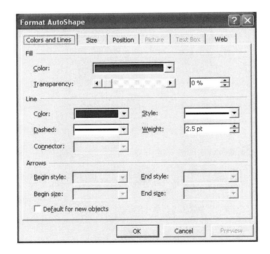

〽 Click on OK.

〽 Click on 📋 .

〽 Click on 📋 .

〽 Drag the pasted shape so that it is adjacent to the first one.

〽 Click on 📋 again and add the next shape. Repeat until you reach the other side of the slide.

The slides should now resemble the one on the CD.

A more sophisticated list

Frankly, the bulleted list can get a bit tedious. So here's one of my alternatives: the thought balloons used in the presentation discussed in the last chapter:

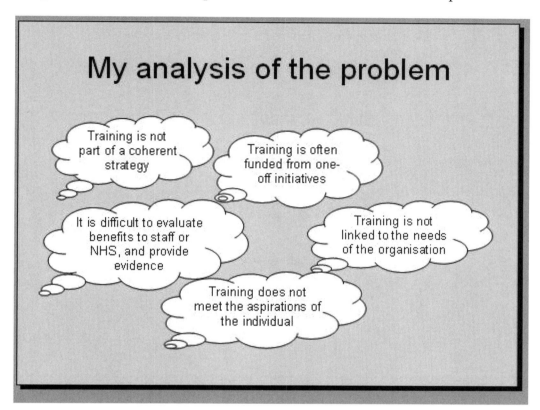

CD link
On the CD you will find the finished slide as 'better-list.ppt' in the Chapter 9 folder.

Start with a new PowerPoint presentation.

Over to you
The first part is by way of revision, so it's over to you.

1   Set the background to a nice plain light blue.
2   Change the slide layout to a simple bulleted list.
3   Delete the bulleted list text box.
4   Type 'My analysis of the problem' as the title.

The result of this is shown below.

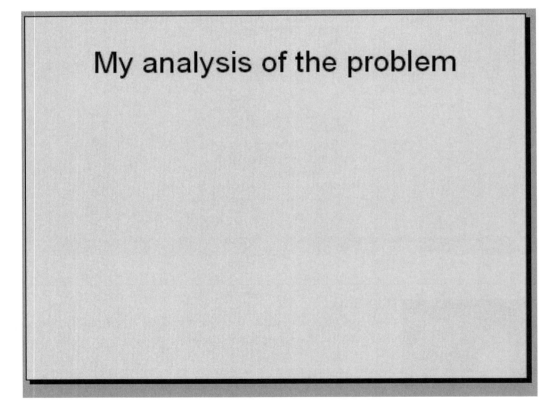

The thought balloons can be found on the Autoshapes menu.

⌐ᵐ   Click on A̲utoshapes.
⌐ᵐ   Click on C̲allouts.
⌐ᵐ   Click on the cloud symbol.

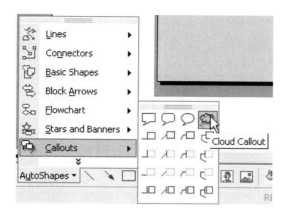

🖐 Drag the shape to a suitable size.

⌨ Type 'Training is not part of a coherent strategy'.

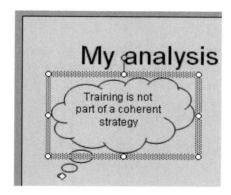

🖐 Right-click on the shape.

🖐 Select Format Autoshape.

🖐 Click on Fill Colour.

🖐 Select white as the fill colour to increase the contrast:

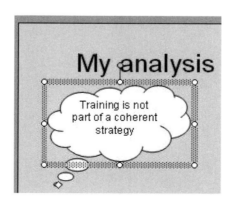

The final stage is to add the transition effect.

- ✓🖑 Click on Slide Show.
- ✓🖑 Click on Custom Animation.

The custom animation dialog appears on the right-hand side of the screen.

- ✓🖑 Click on Add Effect.
- ✓🖑 Click on Entrance
- ✓🖑 Click on 3. Dissolve In.
- ✓🖑 Select On Click as the Start option.

The remaining four thought balloons may be added in similar fashion, so it's over to you.

Over to you
Repeat the process using the following text in the following order:

1 'Training is often funded from one-off initiatives'
2 'Training is not linked to the needs of the organisation'
3 'Training does not meet the aspirations of the individual'
4 'It is difficult to evaluate benefits to staff or NHS, and provide evidence'

The result should be a slide like the one on the CD, shown on page 183.

10

What's on the CD

The CD contains a range of useful resources:

- the text of the book in Acrobat format with colour illustrations
- chapter-specific resources
- templates and designs
- links to useful online resources.

To access the CD, put it in your CD drive.

The following screen should appear, and Alec will be there to greet you!

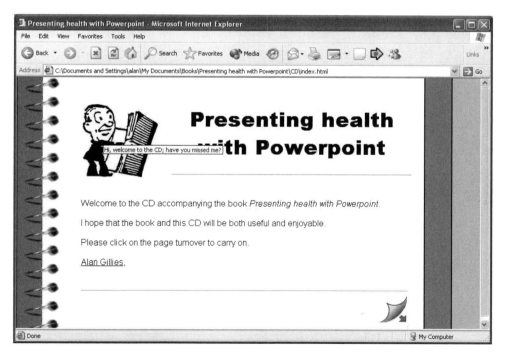

If it doesn't, then click on My Computer on the desktop, and select the CD-ROM drive with the CD in it:

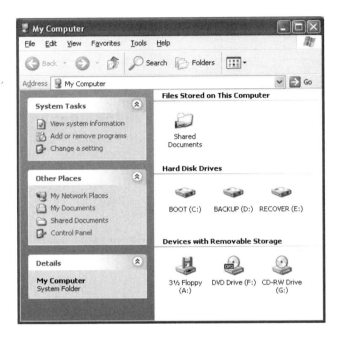

✓☝ Double-click on the correct drive icon.
✓☝ Double-click on index.html.

You should now be at the introductory page of the CD. Click on the turnover to reach the contents page.

Smart Alec says
'Enjoy exploring the CD, but remember you will need an Internet connection to reach the online resources.
   If you like, you can also explore the CD directly from Windows Explorer or My Computer.'

Didn't you just know he'd try and get the final word?

Index

3-D effects 95–6, 143
35mm slides 21

acetates, OHP 21
aide-memoire 146, 149
aims, of talk 147, 149
alignment, text 25
animation effects 39–50
    custom 45–50
    preset 39–45
    slide transitions 41–2, 140, 143
Assistants, Office 31

backgrounds
    black screens 171–3
    busy 139–40
    colour 31–5, 55–6, 77–8
    contrast 138–9
    graded 34–5, 139
    tables 77–8
    textured 35–7, 114–21
black screens 171–3
bold text 25, 26
border effects 95–6
branding 101–7
brick texture 114–21, 159
bullet points 27–8, 146, 163, 165–6
    alternatives 161, 183–6
busy backgrounds 139–40

cartoons 160, 166–7
case, text 137–8
CD contents 187–8

charts 157
    from Excel spreadsheets 80–2
    from Paint application 82–5
checklists 152–4
    PowerPoint 152–3
    talk 153–4
Clip Art
    adding 60–3
    sourcing 109–22
clutter 134–44
colour
    background 31–5, 55–6, 77–8
    presentation rules 138–9
constant headers/footers 159, 163
contrast, text/background 138–9
copy and paste 78–80
curtain calls 173–82

data projectors 21, 22
diagrams, presentation rules 138
digitised photos 89
disappear effect 47–9
display options 21–2

ECDL learning outcomes viii
edit menu 7
effects tip 39
email addresses 159
enhancing talks 146
entertaining the audience 146, 149
entrance effects 91–2, 143
evidence, providing 148, 149–50
examples, presentations 155–69
Excel spreadsheets, charts from 80–2

fading 40–1, 43–4, 46–9
file menu 6
fonts
    appearance 23–7, 159
    mixing 136–7, 157–8
footers/headers, constant 159, 163
format menu 7
formatting
    text 23–9
    whole presentations 29–39

gallery, presentation 155–69
google.com (search engine) 111–14, 121
graded backgrounds 34–5, 139
graphs 80–5, 157

headers/footers, constant 159, 163
help menu 8
hexiplication 146
highway code, information 133–44
house styles 29, 101–7
HTML format 122–9

images
    adding 60–3
    photos 86–9
    sourcing 109–22
information highway code 133–44
internet see World Wide Web
italic text 26

key messages 148, 149
keyboard shortcuts 15

layers 64–5
LCD panels 21
'less is more' rule 134–44
line spacing 28–9
lines, adding 90–2
logos, adding 57–60, 104–5
lower case text 137–8

main window 4
maps, presentation 9–10
master slides 29–39, 55–9, 101–7
menu bar 4
menu structure 5–9
menus, full 6–9
Microsoft PowerPoint website 109–11

mistakes, avoiding 133–44
mixing fonts 136–7, 157–8

new (blank) presentations, opening 19
new presentations, creating 9–15
NHS house styles 104–7
NHSIA website 122

Office Assistants 31
OHP acetates 21
organisational charts 66–71
outline panel 4
outline tab 10
'Over to you' feature vii

party tricks 171–86
paste, copy and 78–80
photos
    adding 86–9
    producing digitised 89
pictures see images; photos
pills images 121
planning presentations 147–51
PowerPoint website 109–11
presentation maps 9–10
presentation rules 134–44
presentations
    examples 155–69
    giving 151–2
    planning 147–51
    viewing 13–14
printing 16–18
problem checks 152–3
projectors, data 21, 22
prototyping 150–1
publishing on the Web 122–9

records, permanent 146, 149
requirements vi
resources
    CD contents 187–8
    World Wide Web 109–29
rules, presentation 134–44

saving presentations 14–15
scanned photos 89
screen layout 3–4
screenshots 165
search engines 111–14, 121

shadowed effect
  photos 88–9
  text 27
shortcut panel 4
shortcuts, keyboard 15
simplicity 133–44
slide masters 29–39, 55–9, 101–7
slide show menu 8
slide transitions 41–2, 140, 143
slides, 35mm 21
'Smart Alec' feature vi–vii
smoking cessation scenario 9–20
sound 96–9
spacing, line 28–9
spellchecking 151–2
status bar 4
summaries, providing 146, 149
system taskbar 4

tables
  background colour 77–8
  copy and paste 78–80
  inserting 71–6
  from Word documents 78–80
'take home' messages 148, 150
talking with PowerPoint 145–54
  talk checklist 153–4
target audiences 147–8, 149
text
  alignment 25
  appearance 23–7, 159
  bold 25, 26
  case 137–8

formatting 23–9
  italic 26
  mixing fonts 136–7, 157–8
  shadowed effect 27
  underlining 26
text boxes 165
  adding 93–6
textured backgrounds 35–7, 114–21
thought bubbles 159, 160
  bullet points alternative 161, 183–6
title bar 4
toolbar 4
toolbar buttons 15, 16
tools menu 8
transitions, slide 41–2, 140, 143

underlining text 26
upper case text 137–8

video 96–9
view menu 7
viewing presentations 13–14
visual illustration 146, 149

Web see World Wide Web
window menu 8
Word documents, pasting from 78–80
World Wide Web 109–29
  Microsoft PowerPoint website 109–11
  as publishing medium 122–9
  sourcing material 109–22

zone functions, initial screen 3–5